Strengthening
the Organizational
Heart

John R. Mott
1865–1955

Strengthening
the Organizational
Heart

15 Timeless Lessons from
Legendary YMCA Leader John R. Mott

Edited by W. Tracy Howe and Nancy Reece

Providence House Publishers
PROVIDENCE PUBLISHING CORPORATION
FRANKLIN, TENNESSEE

Printed in the United States of America

10   09   08   07   06   1   2   3   4   5

Library of Congress Control Number: 2005935677

ISBN: 1-57736-365-5 (hardcover)
ISBN: 1-57736-366-3 (softcover)

Cover design by Joey McNair

Frontispiece photo provided by Kautz Family YMCA Archives, University of Minnesota Libraries.

The poem on page 137, "An Indispensable Man" by Saxon White Kessinger © 1959, is used by permission. All rights reserved.

Scripture quotations marked "HCSB" are taken from the Holman Christian Standard Bible®. Copyright© 1999, 2000, 2002, 2003 by Holman Bible Publishers. Used by permission.
Scripture quotations marked "KJV" are taken from the Holy Bible, King James Version, Cambridge, 1769.
Scripture quotations marked "NASB" are taken from the New American Standard Bible®. Copyright© 1960, 1962, 1963, 1971, 1972, 1973, 1975, 1977, 1995 by The Lockman Foundation. Used by permission.
Scripture quotations marked "NCV" are taken from the New Century Version®. Copyright© 1987, 1988, 1991 by Thomas Nelson Inc. Used by permission. All rights reserved.
Scripture quotations marked "NIV" are taken from HOLY BIBLE, NEW INTERNATIONAL VERSION®. Copyright©1973, 1978, 1984 by International Bible Society. Used by permission of Zondervan Publishing House.
Scripture quotations marked "NLT" are taken from the Holy Bible, New Living Translation, copyright 1996. Used by permission of Tyndale House Publishers, Inc., Wheaton, Illinois 60189. All rights reserved.
Scripture quotations marked "NKJV" are taken from The New King James Version/Thomas Nelson Publishers, Nashville: Thomas Nelson Publishers. Copyright© 1982. Used by permission. All rights reserved.
Scripture quotations marked "NRSV" are taken from The Holy Bible: New Revised Standard Version/Division of Christian Education of the National Council of Churches of Christ in the United States of America.—Nashville: Thomas Nelson Publishers, © 1989. Used by permission. All rights reserved.
Scripture quote on page 153 is taken from The Message by Eugene H. Peterson, copyright © 1993, 1994, 1995, 1996, 2000, 2001, 2002. Used by permission of NavPress Publishing Group. All rights reserved.

PROVIDENCE HOUSE PUBLISHERS
an imprint of
Providence Publishing Corporation
238 Seaboard Lane • Franklin, Tennessee 37067
www.providence-publishing.com
800-321-5692

CONTENTS

FOREWORD

When I was a youngster growing up in New Rochelle, New York, the YMCA was central to my life. We hung out there, swam there, played church league basketball there, and generally, grew up there. It was a place that welcomed us all.

Looking back on those experiences, the only regret I have is that our Y never taught us about Jesus. He seemed to take a back seat to being a wonderful community center. That is sad because Jesus is the master of the art of living and the art of leadership. And yet too many organizations founded on Christian principles have turned their backs on their competitive edge—Jesus. It does not have to be that way in the future if *Strengthening the Organizational Heart* is distributed, read, and taught to every member in every YMCA everywhere, as well as in other Christian-based organizations.

This wonderful book contains "Fifteen Timeless Lessons from Legendary YMCA Leader John R. Mott," with heartfelt commentary from sixteen dedicated leaders in the YMCA movement.

It is no accident that the first timeless lesson that Mott shared is:

Jesus Christ is the Foundation. He provides the direction and the zest for life. If we understand his teachings and his personality, he will make his own impression on our lives and it will be revolutionary.

That word "revolutionary" is powerful. What does it mean? It means if we study the life and teachings of Jesus of Nazareth, it could change our lives, whether we be a YMCA leader, a member, or somebody trying to run a values-driven organization or family.

We are reminded that in all relationships, change is the constant. Nowhere is this more true than our relationship with God. Do I love Him more now, mid-morning, than I did at dawn today? Do I rely on Him more surely at this time in my life than when I was a teenager? Am I seeking His will and serving Him with an ever-more-widely-open heart?

Studying the life and teachings of Jesus that Mott and other leaders of the YMCA movement share will give you the guidance you need to answer those questions. As Mott says,

> Religious truth was not intended merely to be contemplated: it was designed to be done. Our moral and religious life is not a train of thoughts but a life of action, of constant exertion of the will.

If you want to make your life better—and the lives of those you touch in your organizations, at work, at home, and in the community—you will find this book a gift. Not only is there much wisdom contained herein, there is also the spirit that comes with the recognition that serving Him and serving others introduces us to an unsurpassable sweetness. What could be greater than that?

Ken Blanchard
Co-author *The One Minute Manager*®
and *Lead Like Jesus*

ACKNOWLEDGMENTS

The editors and contributors are indebted to many individuals who assisted in the development of *Strengthening the Organizational Heart.*

They gratefully acknowledge **Fiona Soltes** for her contributions of vision, insight, and talent in making this a book that captures the heart of the YMCA;

Dagmar Getz of the Kautz Family YMCA Archives at the University of Minnesota in Minneapolis, who assisted in selecting photographic images of Mott;

Martha Lund Smalley, research services librarian and curator of the Day Missions Collection at the Yale University Divinity School Library, which houses the John R. Mott Collection, and who provided important information about Mott materials;

John Harr, associate university librarian, Vanderbilt University, who made available numerous volumes by Mott housed in the Vanderbilt University Divinity Library collections;

James White, senior vice president of leadership development at the YMCA of the Triangle, for support encouragement, and consultation;

Dottie Hamilt, **Nancy Jordan**, and **Martha Lawrence** of Blanchard Training and Development; **Shane Benson** of Chick-fil-A Inc., and **Jim Greene** of Matthews, North Carolina, for their assistance in obtaining editorial contributions; and, especially,

Publisher **Andrew Miller** and his staff, including Copyeditor **Kelly Bainbridge**, Production Manager **Holly Jones**, Designer **Joey McNair**, Production Editor **Tammy Spurlock**, and Managing Editor **Nancy Wise**, who all worked enthusiastically to take this project from concept to reality.

ix

INTRODUCTION

Movies are such a powerful way to communicate a message. One movie which carries a poignant message is titled *Dead Poets Society* and stars Robin Williams as a teacher in a prestigious all boys' prep school.

On the first day of class, this new teacher entered the classroom with his class of about twenty boys. After taking roll, he walked out into the hallway, signaling to the boys to follow him out of the classroom. One by one they apprehensively got up from their seats and moved into the hallway nervously looking at one another. As they sheepishly looked around, the teacher, Mr. Keating, drew their attention to a wall covered with the pictures of the classes of students who had graced the halls since the school's inception. The school's long history was evident by the number of pictures. The rich tradition of the school was obvious. Mr. Keating said, "Look at the faces of these boys. They were once just like you—full of life and hormones; but now they are all gone—food for worms. Listen to their voices calling to you from the grave." Again, the boys grinned nervously, but they looked into the eyes of those who had preceded them and scanned the faces. They looked at each face wondering what these boys would say to them. At that point, Mr. Keating softly breathed the words, "Carpe diem," and then a pause, and again, "Carpe diem." And one last whisper, "Make your lives extraordinary."

The authors of these essays believe that if we were able to hear the voices of our predecessors in the YMCA, we might hear the same message. Voices like those of George Williams, Luther Gulick, D. L. Moody, James Naismith, John R. Mott, and all of those who are a part of the YMCA Hall of Fame would call out to us loudly, "Carpe diem" or seize the day.

Fortunately, John R. Mott has left us with some additional wisdom by means of fifteen very practical principles which give us insight into what he would say to us from the grave. Near the end of his life he put pen to those things that he felt he had learned as a result of his many decades of service to the YMCA.

If we can read and digest these principles, we will have the advantage of adding Mott's accumulated knowledge to our own. It's amazing how eternal these principles still are. We have the benefit of measuring them against our own experience all of these years later.

As you read these chapters written by YMCA leaders from around the United States, the hope is that you will find a greater depth of understanding into the mind of John R. Mott and into the truth of those principles he deemed to be of the greatest importance.

—Eric Ellsworth

JOHN R. MOTT
A Man With Vision for All Time

Centuries ago, when men of faith compiled the stories, teachings, and experiences that we would come to know as the Bible, they must have understood that they were part of something much larger than themselves.

There are moments, after all, that can only be God-appointed. There are truths that can only remain timeless. And there are people who somehow innately understand how to pull back the curtain and see into the very heart of their Creator.

John R. Mott was one of those people. His name may not be as familiar as that of, say, Billy Graham or Oswald Chambers, but the imprint of his life has been no less compelling. Now, before you say he was another man for another time—he died in 1955, after all—consider his thoughts on the state of the "current" world:

> Throughout the world there is a sense of insecurity and instability. Ancient religions are undergoing modification, and in some regions dissolution, as scientific and commercial development alter the current of men's thought. Institutions regarded with age-long veneration are discarded or called in question; well-established standards of moral conduct are brought under criticism; and countries called Christian feel the stress as truly as the peoples of Asia and Africa. On all sides doubt is expressed whether there is any absolute truth or goodness. A new relativism struggles to enthrone itself in human thought.
>
> Along with this is found the existence of world-wide suffering and pain, which expresses itself partly in a despair of all higher values, partly in a tragically earnest quest of a new basis for life and thought, in the

birthpangs of rising nationalism, in the ever-keener consciousness of race- and class-oppression.

Amid widespread indifference and immersion in material concerns we also find everywhere, now in noble forms and now in license or extravagance, a great yearning, especially among the youth of the world, for the full and untrammeled expression of personality, for spiritual leadership and authority, for reality in religion, for social justice, for human brotherhood, for international peace.

Sound familiar? Mott said then—as he would today, were he still alive—that the answer to all of it was simply Jesus Christ. Led by biblical principles and guided by the Spirit, Mott was not simply a man with vision of his time. He was a man with vision for all time.

Mott spoke those words in 1928. But as we continue to face some of the same issues he faced then, his vision remains one worth catching. Through his life as an evangelist, author, Nobel Peace Prize winner, and former president of the YMCA's World Committee, he advocated simple, timeless truths that changed the environment around him. They included, for example, keeping Jesus as the foundation of all things, promoting the study of the Bible, understanding the power of prayer, and paying special attention to groups like youth and the elderly.

These ideas provided a backbone for the eloquent and inspirational speeches Mott gave throughout his life. When he was in his eighties, he addressed the Enlarged Executive Committee of the World's Committee of the YMCA in Geneva, Switzerland, and in that talk, presented a specific, extended list of principles or "fundamental processes" for living the godly life. Those principles are as relevant as ever.

They're especially relevant within the YMCA. It was Mott's involvement in the Young Men's Christian

Association as a young adult that helped spark the fire that burned so brightly. Mott attended a Dwight Moody summer conference for young men in 1886, and was compelled by the enthusiasm for foreign missions that was in the air. Not long after, he became president of the Cornell University YMCA, turning it into the world's largest and most active student association. From there, he went on to integrate the lively Student Volunteer Movement into the Y and traveled the globe to help create the World Student Christian Federation. He became chairman of the Edinburgh World Missionary Conference in 1910, General Secretary of the American YMCA, and chairman of its National War Work Council, as well as chairman of the International Missionary Council. By the time he earned the Nobel Peace Prize in 1946, he was cited for his "earnest and undiscourage-able effort to weave together all nations, all races, and all religious communions in friendliness, in fellowship, and in cooperation."

And yet, he remained a humble servant who simply sought God for direction, and then was faithful to do what God said.

Maybe you've known someone like Mott in your life-time, someone who lived and breathed to be in the very center of God's will, to be pleasing to God's heart. Christian organizations like the YMCA are fortunate to find such people among their staff and volunteers. Such people see their involvement not as a job, but as a true calling by God and a chance to affect eternity.

You'll meet a few of these people in the pages of this book. They've been leaders, they've been followers, and they've been servants, laying everything on the line for the causes they believe in. The individual YMCAs with which they're involved have caught their fire and vision, and have set standards not only as organizations that change the lives of those around them, but also as true Christian entities that aren't afraid to openly stand on the firm foundations of faith.

For these leaders, Mott's principles are not simply "good ideas." They are instead a way of living everyday life, as comfortable and familiar as a well-worn Bible at the bedside. You'll see that in the way they've taken each of Mott's lessons and illuminated them with present-day stories. That's the thing about timeless truth, after all. It stands for generations, carries on for centuries, and still has the power to compel and inspire us.

Consider then, making their words—and Mott's principles—your own. Be it 1886 or 2006, God remains the same yesterday, today, and forever. And we, too, by answering His call, are given the opportunity to take part in something larger than ourselves.

LESSONS I HAVE LEARNED
by John R. Mott

After a lifetime in Christian work and extensive travel in eighty-three nations, I would suggest for your consideration, fifteen basic lessons that I have learned:

1. **Jesus Christ Is the Foundation.** He provides the direction and the zest for life. If we understand his teachings and his personality, he will make his own impression on our lives and it will be revolutionary.

2. **Rule by the Heart.** People are reached "via the heart." There is no substitute for love and kindness and sympathy.

3. **Study Priorities.** No man can do all the good to be done in the world. We need to list and study our own priorities daily.

4. **We Can Trust Others.** We can afford great acts of trust. I can testify that I have never had others disappoint me.

5. **Study and Promote the Use of the Bible.** De Quincey said the cause of all evil is the lack of interest in religious writing. If I were to stay longer, I would give a frontline place to reawakening interest in the religious writings of Christianity. There is nothing to take their place.

6. **The Discipline of Prayer Is Essential.** "He departed a stone's cast beyond the Apostles, and kneeled down and prayed." I need only to say that we must make prayer one of the primary objectives of this brotherhood.

7. **Do "Multiplying" Work.** "He that does the work is not as profitably employed as he who multiplies the doers." Enlisting volunteers is one of our greatest tasks.

8. **Use the "Heroic Appeal."** A heroic appeal often gets a heroic response. It is good to have difficulties because it calls out the most in you, it drives you to get the cooperation of others, it drives you to God.

9. **Strategy Is Important.** There are strategic points which if captured, make easy all that lies behind them. There are strategic classes and strategic races, strategic times, strategic methods, strategic places. We must know what they are.

10. **We Need to Get into the Field.** You cannot develop a Christian from an office chair. We need to be out meeting and dealing with personalities.

11. **Small Groups Are of Great Value.** Christ sent them out "two by two." At one time, he had five disciples, at another time three, another time eleven, and at another, twelve. Why did Christ attach importance to small groups? I long ago decided that it was wise to follow Christ in this method.

12. **Adolescence Is a Crucial Time.** If I had my life to live over I would spend much time on the adolescents' age group. These are the habit-forming years, the years of determining life attitude and tendencies, the years of creativeness.

13. **Don't Overlook Old People.** Here is wisdom and experience for our asking. Here, also, is a group to whom we must give kindness and affection.

14. **Emphasize the Immediate.** We need to live under the spell of immediacy. What other time will there be? What other generations than the present can we work with?

15. **Be Attentive unto God.** "Speak Lord, for thy servant hearkens," and "My soul, be silent unto God," say what I mean. We must put out other sounds—noises of selfish ambition—prepare ourselves to say, "Speak Lord, for thy servant hearkens."

—From remarks presented at the
North American Association of YMCA
Secretaries meeting, May 25, 1948
Grand Rapids, Michigan

Strengthening the Organizational Heart

1

Jesus Christ is the Foundation

He provides the direction and the zest for life.
If we understand his teachings and his personality,
he will make his own impression on our lives
and it will be revolutionary.

JRM

by Dick Marks

Five years invested, and for what?

Nothing but a lesson that shook me to the core.

It's been more than thirty years since it happened, but I can still feel the shame as if it were yesterday. At the time, I was serving as the YMCA's youth outreach director in Westfield, Massachusetts. I was able to develop significant relationships with some of the nontraditional teens who had found a home at our downtown coffeehouse and felt I was making a difference. Then, in the spring of 1975, I accepted the position of executive director at the YMCA in Waynesboro, Pennsylvania, and I had to leave these good friends behind. There were several memorable and tearful good-byes, but none I remember more than my final get-together with the kids who had been part of the coffeehouse leadership.

We met in the youth center of the Y and exchanged warm stories about adventures we had shared over the years. A lot of "remember when . . ." tales were passed around, and then, in my final words with the kids, I spoke of my personal faith in Christ and how I

3

had tried to serve Jesus as I worked with them. When I finished, I felt that I had expressed my faith and motivations clearly.

As the meeting broke up, one of the teens came to me, gave me a hug, and said, "Dick, I was surprised to hear what you said tonight about Jesus. I thought you were just a nice guy."

"A nice guy." The words still sting. My investment in these kids brought the credit to me as a "nice guy" rather than to the Lord of my life. Right then, I made a commitment to God that I would never again be shy about making the foundations of my faith known.

A Secure Foundation

Ever been there? Ever had a moment when you knew there was something more you could say, but didn't? A Scripture you could offer, but chose not to? A prayer that could be shared, but wasn't? All of those things show others who we are—and how much of Christ we're willing to let the world see.

I use a personal example here because organizations are made of individuals and those individuals help lay a foundation that can make a significant impact on the lives of the people around them.

For more than 150 years, the YMCA has emphasized the importance of a secure foundation. And just as John R. Mott, a YMCA hero from another generation, has proclaimed, that foundation is Jesus Christ.

Mott was a dynamic leader with a high-impact personality. But his expression of faith developed over time. He wasn't always open about his convictions. In his early youth, he had been quiet about faith issues. Then in the fall of 1883, Mott was introduced to the YMCA chapter at Upper Iowa University. At the university, Mott said, God moved him "to live an open, active, religious life." He came out of his spiritual closet to use his gifts to draw others to Christ. As far as he was concerned, "The Christians of this generation are to give every person of this age an opportunity to accept Jesus Christ." He was a man with a growing faith and whose life was an exciting mission that touched many.

And that spark was ignited with the help of the Y.

At the YMCA, we're blessed to work under an ideological umbrella that not only allows but actually calls for a Christ-centered foundation. The very Statement of Purpose of the National Constitution of the YMCA says this: "The Young Men's Christian Association we regard as being in its essential genius a worldwide fellowship united by a common loyalty to Jesus Christ for the purpose of developing Christian personality and building a Christian society." This mission statement is so central to the movement that every YMCA director must, by personal signature, acknowledge acceptance and support of the statement each year in order to have their local Y credentialed by the YMCA of the USA. We have the historic base on which to stand for Jesus Christ and His redeeming power and love. What does that stand look like when it's fleshed out at a particular Y?

That all depends on the individuals involved. It might even depend on you.

Feet Firmly Planted

Because each Y is autonomous and should be reflective of its own community, the Christ-centered basis can be expected to look different in each locale. A Bible in the lobby may be appropriate in Waynesboro, Pennsylvania, but it might be inappropriate in the predominantly Jewish city of Newton, Massachusetts. But even in Waynesboro, where the community expects the Y to have strong Christian emphasis, such faith-based evidence is not likely to be seen without committed Christian leadership in place to encourage it. Jesus Christ must be the personal foundation for the leaders of the organization before such a spiritual purpose is intentionally and clearly revealed in the organization. It doesn't matter what principles or mission statements are written to establish and guide the organization. Eventually, the YMCA—or any other organization, for that matter—will reflect the commitments and foundations of its leaders.

> **"Jesus Christ . . . is incomparably the greatest leader** the world has ever known. . . . Therefore, the supremely important thing in the discovery, development, and enlargement of the highest leadership so much needed the world over, is a growing acquaintance and a deepening fellowship with this Central Figure of the Ages and the Eternities."[1]   **JRM**

Throughout this book, you'll hear from Y leaders with solid foundations, those who have been willing to let their commitments be seen. And, in between the lines, you'll see faith in action, prayers answered, and God glorified, all because these individuals have been willing to plant their feet firmly on those foundations while they reach out to others.

One of those is Billy Sievers, and he's a great place to start.

Billy, a lively, energetic twelve-year-old, never met Tom Balistrere, but if he had, he would have liked him. And, in turn, Tom would have been proud of Billy, who graciously accepted the Waynesboro YMCA's Balistrere Sportsmanship Award from Charlene, Tom's widow. Billy received the accolade because he exemplifies the character values that Tom stood for in the community.

Tom Balistrere was a strong figure in the small Pennsylvania community just north of the Mason-Dixon Line, and he was known for much more than his character. Most everyone in Waynesboro knew Tom. Some knew him as "Mr. B.," the good-natured high school science teacher, but those who played basketball for him called him "Coach." However you greeted him, though,

Tom probably knew your name and your mother's name, and had an encouraging word, humorous story, and gentle smile for you. He left you feeling better about yourself and about life, and as such, kids loved being around him.

Shortly after coming to Waynesboro, Tom started the community youth basketball program, which he soon brought to the YMCA. Coach B was at his best when he was teaching the fundamentals of the game he loved. "To shoot a basketball," Tom would tell the kids, "Remember the BEEF—Balance, Eye, Elbow, and Follow-Through." "If you don't start with the right balance," Tom would say, as he dramatically planted his feet, "nothing else will work. You've got to start with the right foundation."

If Billy Sievers had known Tom before a sudden heart attack felled him, he would have learned that Tom had his priorities clear in basketball and in life. He taught kids that to succeed in life, you have to have your priorities right. You've got to put God first, then family, then school, and then basketball. When he said it, the kids listened with interest because they knew he cared about them and they saw him live the principles he taught. His foundation was solid, and it was this: Jesus Christ was the first priority.

Tom purchased a large Bible for the Y lobby, and it's still there today, providing wisdom to people of all ages and faiths. For some Y members, stopping to read a verse from Tom's Bible is a daily ritual.

Facing Adversity With Strength

For many, Tom Balistrere was a role model. He, John R. Mott, and many other successful Christian leaders of our time have recognized that a life built upon Jesus Christ can withstand the buffeting of the world's tests and temptations. The challenges of sickness, death, broken relationships, financial stress, and harsh criticism can shake even a veteran leader, and the allure of position, wealth, and immorality has taken many down. But Mott knew that with Christ as his cornerstone, he could face such adversities and seductions with strength.

> **"He [Christ] imparts a sense of mission which** surmounts all difficulties, opposition, discouragement, and loneliness. To Him we go for those guiding principles which, when resolutely and courageously applied, solve life's problems and effect revolutionary and trans-forming changes."[2] **JRM**

As Mott matured in his faith, he continued to rise to leadership positions. In fact, he had to make some difficult choices about how he would use his God-given gifts. Early in his career, President Woodrow Wilson asked him to take over the presidency of Princeton University, and later, to become the nation's first ambassador to China. While either offer would have guaranteed Mott great prestige, he rejected them both. His commitment to his faith compelled him to pursue his calling to leadership in lesser-known but more spiritual ventures. He made his decisions from a solid foundation on Jesus Christ.

Mott saw his calling this way: "The supreme purpose of the Christian church is to make Jesus Christ known, trusted, loved, obeyed and exemplified in the whole range of an individual's life—body, mind and spirit—and also in all human relationships. This is incomparably the most important work for every Christian." Through his personal faith, Mott found great purpose for his life.

First Things First

These days, the idea of purpose in life can be synonymous with a popular book by Rick Warren. *The Purpose-Driven Life* topped the *New York Times* best-seller list for many weeks. With more than thirty million copies sold, it earned the distinction of being one of the highest-selling books in publishing history. Warren recognizes the preeminent importance of a sound base by beginning his treatise with a chapter titled "It All Starts with God." On the very first page, he establishes priorities by saying that we must "begin with God."

"You were born by His purpose and for His purpose," he writes. So it is for us. Nothing short of a foundation built on Jesus Christ will stabilize our lives and give meaning to our work for the YMCA and other faith-based organizations.

Rick Warren certainly didn't make this discovery first. God Himself identified the principle, and Jesus reinforced it in the Great Commandment. When asked to identify the greatest of the Mosaic laws, Jesus answered, "You must love the Lord your God with all your heart, all your soul, and all your mind" (Matt. 22:37 NLT). Jesus also made the importance of a proper foundation clear in His teaching about those who build houses on rock and sand.

Even the secular world has acknowledged that there is power in a godly perspective. Emphasis by government leaders on "faith-based" programs recognizes that a godly basis gives opportunity for dealing with the total person—spirit, mind, and body—and achieving results that are otherwise unattainable. The dramatic successes of many of these programs, particularly in dealing with addictions, demonstrate the power of a solid foundation on God. The track records of Alcoholics Anonymous and Teen Challenge stand as prime examples. Such faith-based organizations record success rates more than five times greater than their secular counterparts. So the successful life starts with the proper spiritual base, but for those of us who have already made Jesus Christ our foundation, God expects more.

Jesus asks us to serve God and to lead an exemplary life, but He also tells us that we should reveal the source of the strength that enables us to live a good life. He put it this way: "Let your light so shine before men, that they may see your good works and glorify your Father in heaven" (Matt. 5:16 NKJV). God wants us to give testimony to His life in us and to point others to Him. He wants the credit for the successes in our lives.

> **"If we would have the true idea and spirit of Christian** leadership, we must study with diligence the life of that Leader of leaders, as clearly set forth in the Scriptures."[3]
>
> **JRM**

In organizations like the YMCA, there's both a call and an opportunity for a staff member or volunteer to be a loving witness for Jesus. To do so first requires a solid personal foundation on Christ, plus the commitment to live a life that gives God the glory. Such a lifestyle will then encourage the Billy Sieverses of our communities to want to live by the priorities that we model. This is stable, powerful leadership that attracts others, builds heroes, and leaves living legacies that glorify God and expand His kingdom. It's a grand calling and purpose. Being simply a "nice guy" doesn't even come close.

LESSON 1
IN REFLECTION
For Yourself

1. What are the top five priorities in your life?
2. Describe a time when your priorities helped you make a difficult decision.
3. Which of the choices below best describes your willingness to discuss your faith?
   - A. My faith is private and personal. I don't discuss it with others.
   - B. I will discuss my faith if asked.
   - C. I look for opportunities to talk about my faith with people I know.
   - D. I am proactive about sharing my faith, even with strangers.

For Group Discussion and Leadership

1. If a donor asked you to describe the foundation of your organization, how would you respond? How do the values of Jesus affect your organization?
2. The book *Good to Great* taught the importance of preserving the core of an organization. What is the core of your organization?
3. How does your organization reflect the commitments and foundation of your leaders?
4. What does a Christ–centered basis for your organization look like in your community?

2

Rule by the Heart

People are reached "via the heart." There is no substitute for love and kindness and sympathy.
JRM

by Nancy Reece

It was a cold, snowy, and very dark night in the middle of downtown Chicago. We were walking along a sidewalk, the skies spitting snow, our cold hands stuffed in our pockets despite wearing gloves. The slush on the sides of the street had refrozen into a gray, dingy mass of cold ice, and each step had to be taken carefully to avoid a slip.

We were returning to our apartment just north of downtown when we saw a man lying in the middle of the sidewalk about two blocks in front of us. As we approached, we noticed people gingerly stepping around him or going into—or even across—the street to avoid getting too close.

In the city, you have to have your street smarts, and know enough to make sure you're not going to be set up as a victim. But in this case, the man was conscious, obviously in pain, and also obviously drunk. We knew, as we approached, that we had to do something.

My husband bent down and gently asked the man what was wrong. He had slipped on the ice, wrenched his knee, and couldn't walk. We suspected he was homeless. And then an interesting thing happened. Within two minutes of my husband and I stopping to assist this man, other people began approaching to help. A woman came from across the street.

"I was watching him for the last thirty minutes from my apartment up there," she said, pointing up to a lighted window across the street. "I was wondering if anyone would help him." Someone else used a cell phone to call for an ambulance, and within ten minutes, the homeless man was on his way to medical attention. And as for us, as we went on our own way, we wondered why no one had been willing to stop and be the first to help their fellow human being in need.

We decided they were ruled by fear. But as Christians, we are commanded by Jesus in John 14:27, "Do not let your heart be troubled, nor let it be fearful" (NASB). We are to rule by the heart.

John R. Mott's basic lesson of "rule by the heart" seems at first glance a simple one. He reminds us to treat people with love, kindness, and sympathy. That's good advice. We live in a world, after all, that demands that we as Christians walk the talk . . . or else tarnish Christ's name. The words "hypocrite," "charlatan," and "fake" are sometimes used by the world when describing Christians. So, how do we make a difference? Through love.

To Rule by the Heart, Guard Your Heart

Let's start with a look at Proverbs 4:23: "Above all else, guard your heart, for it affects everything you do" (NLT). But, what exactly is meant by a well-guarded heart? Part of that has to do with what should be kept in, and part of it, what should be kept out. Consider the heart that is not well-guarded. A search through Scriptures paints a picture of this heart: one without the saving faith of Jesus Christ.

- "For out of the heart come evil thoughts, murders, adulteries, fornications, thefts, false witness, slander" (Matt. 15:19 NASB).
- "The LORD said to himself . . . 'the intent of man's heart is evil from his youth'"(Gen. 8:21 NASB).

- "Deceit is in the heart of those who devise evil" (Prov. 12:20 NASB).

That depicts a dark and miserable picture, much like Dickens described Scrooge in *A Christmas Carol:* "A squeezing, wrenching, grasping, scarping, clutching covetous old sinner. Hard and sharp as flint, from which no steel had ever struck out generous fire; secret, and self-contained, and solitary as an oyster."

No wonder Scrooge was a covetous old sinner, and no wonder the people on the streets of Chicago passed by a man in need. We live in a world that doesn't celebrate people who rule by the heart; it celebrates those whose hearts are darkened by fortune, fame, passion, and power.

In contrast, the well-guarded heart is one that loves. In John Mott's own words, the well-guarded heart becomes a repository for the Word, a place for secret prayer, and a vessel for the "morning watch," (the practice of spending the first half hour of every day in personal devotion).

> **"Our true and compelling motive lies in the very** nature of the God to whom we have given our hearts. Since He is love, His very nature is to share."[1]   **JRM**

"The central thought in all, which should be kept central with us all, is that of the deepening acquaintance with God and the releasing of His superhuman guidance and power through right habits of isolation, mediation, communion, and appropriation," Mott wrote in *That the World May Believe.*

Additionally, if you want to guard your heart well, you have to have a plan. I was stuck in an airport one day. Looking for something to read, I wandered into one of the bookstores and perused the titles on display. My heart leapt as I noticed a book titled *When Women Long for Rest.* I bought it, but it turned out not to be a book you can read quickly. It forced me to ask questions about why I longed for rest and how to change that through study, prayer, and quiet.

The book was so good that I decided to order copies for all the women executives on our staff. The books sat on my table as I took the time to write personal notes to give along with them. Every woman who entered my office and saw the title exhaled and asked for a copy. I had to ask myself: Why do we neglect the soul food we so long for? Why don't we guard our hearts well?

Try this practical test for determining the condition of your heart. It is adapted from the work of John R. Mott himself, and from Bill Hybels, pastor of the Willow Creek Community Church in Chicago. Ask yourself:

1. Do you commit time each day to the study of the Word? It is through study that we learn and understand the heart of God and of Christ. It is also through study that we learn how to rule by the heart—and what love, kindness, and sympathy look like in action. Psalm 119:11 tells us, "I have treasured your word in my heart so that I may not sin against you" (HCSB).

2. Do you spend time each day talking to God? Secret prayer results in many fruits that will enable us to rule by the heart. They include, for example:

   A. *Humility.* "Take my yoke upon you, and learn from Me, for I am gentle and humble in heart, and you shall find rest for your souls" (Matt. 11:29 NASB).

   B. *Purity.* "Blessed are the pure in heart, for they shall see God" (Matt. 5:8 NASB).

   C. *Contrition.* "The sacrifices of God are a broken spirit, a broken and contrite heart . . ." (Ps. 51:17 NASB).

   D. *Peace.* "Be anxious for nothing, but in everything by prayer and supplication with thanksgiving let your request be made known to God. And the peace of God, which surpasses all comprehension, will guard your hearts and your minds in Christ Jesus" (Phil. 4:6–7 NASB).

3. Have you considered taking part in the morning watch? This is perhaps the hardest of Mott's three disciplines. In addition to your study and prayer, do you also simply spend time in quiet before the Lord? As Henri Nouwen so eloquently stated in *The Only Necessary Thing*, "This asks for much discipline and risk taking because we always seem to have something more urgent to do. Just 'sitting there' and 'doing nothing' often disturbs us more than it helps. But there is no way around this. Being useless and silent before God belongs to the core of all prayer."

"Listen to your heart," he continued. "It's there that Jesus speaks most intimately to you. Praying is first and foremost listening to Jesus, who dwells in the very depths of your heart."

4. Can you feel deep emotion? Or are you numb when a tragedy happens to someone? One of the reasons I chose to leave YMCA service in the inner city was that my heart was becoming numb. When incidents of abuse or violence occurred, it was just another day in the projects for me.

5. Are you mindful of moments? Do you see the sunset? A bird in the tree? A child peeping around the corner of a restaurant booth? Do you see the quiet smile of the volunteer you just recognized?

6. Do you experience spontaneity, fun, and laughter? If you're so intense that you aren't having fun in life—using the laughter God created within you—slow down and rediscover this joy.

7. Do you hear God's whispers? Making choices to be still, to be quiet, to pause, enable us to hear those small whispers from our Lord that give us wisdom, insight, and truth.

Guarding our hearts in this way, through study, prayer, quiet, and monitoring our hearts' condition, produces the results that John Mott advocated: ruling by the heart. "For God sees not as man sees, for man looks at the outward appearance, but the Lord looks at the heart," as it says in 1 Samuel 16:7b (NASB).

Loving Our Neighbors

So who are we to look at as the Lord does? Who are we to love? In Luke 10:27, Jesus commanded us to love our neighbor. Then the lawyer asks Jesus "And who is my neighbor?" Jesus responds with the story of the Good Samaritan, which illustrated that the men of God (the priest and the Levite) did not have God's heart, but a man who did not know God (the Samaritan) showed more mercy to the injured man. Even today, we need to ask, "Who is my neighbor?" As Spencer Perkins and Chris Rice write in *More Than Equals*:

> It doesn't take much for each of us to figure out who Jesus would use as an example of "neighbor" in our own towns and cities.
> - For an Israeli, how about a Palestinian?
> - For an Arab, how about a Jew?
> - For a rich white man, how about a black welfare mother?
> - For a poor white, how about a middle-class black who got where he is through affirmative action?
> - For a black male, how about a white male— better yet, a pickup-driving, gun-rack-toting, tobacco-chewing, baseball-cap-wearing white man who still refers to a black man as "boy"?
> - For a feminist, how about an insensitive, domineering male chauvinist?
> - For all of us, how about the unmotivated, undisciplined, uneducated poor or an AIDs victim who contracted AIDs not through a

transfusion but through homosexual activity
or intravenous drug use?

Who would Jesus use as the neighbor if He were
speaking to you?

If we are to rule by the heart, we can't let outward
appearances blind us to the person inside. I learned this
lesson the hard way. I was flying to San Diego and took my
seat on the airplane next to a scruffy-looking teenager. His
pants hung on his hips, his layered shirts were wrinkled
and mismatched, he hadn't shaved in several days, and he
was listening to a CD player on headphones. I wrote him
off as someone I'd have little opportunity to talk to or to
share the gospel with.

But as the flight progressed and the attendants
began to serve lunch, I watched him open a briefcase to
put his headphones in. Much to my surprise, inside the
briefcase was a Bible. To my chagrin, I learned the
young man was a twenty-six-year-old itinerant evangelist flying to work with teens in San Diego. He was
dressed as he was so they would relate to him better. As
we flew across the country, we discussed the four views
of Revelation. God used this to teach me a huge lesson
in judging others—for I had judged on appearance, like
man does, rather than by the heart, as God does. I saw
then that my heart needed to be more aligned with His;
that's the only thing that enables us to love our neighbors and rule by the heart.

Loving Our Enemies and the Lost

We need to remember that the category of our neighbors also includes our enemies and those who persecute
us. It's not so difficult to love those who care for us. "If
you love those who love you, what credit is that to you?"
we're asked in Luke 6:32. "For even sinners love those
who love them" (NASB). That puts a different spin on
love, doesn't it? How do we love a terrorist who beheads
a man to generate fear? Jesus calls us to pray.

What about closer to home? What about the driver who cuts us off at the red light? What about the person at work who undermines you because he or she wants your job? The gossip who spreads lies about you? The atheist who wants Christ out of Christmas? Is your first reaction to these souls one of compassion and mercy? Is your first reaction one of prayer?

The entire book of Jonah teaches us lessons about having a heart for the lost and our enemies. Jonah is called by God to prophesy to Israel's enemies, the Ninevites. Jonah runs away from God's call, puts others at risk, and declares his preference to die rather than to obey God. But he's given a second chance by God, and goes to Nineveh to speak God's Word. Good heavens, the Ninevites actually repent and listen to God. And what does Jonah do? He gets angry because God doesn't destroy Nineveh: "I knew you were compassionate and merciful. I knew you'd make me look like a fool. I knew you'd relent. So take my life!" God asks Jonah if he has reason to be angry. Jonah doesn't respond and gets angry again when God removes the vine he'd provided for Jonah's protection. God then asks Jonah, if he has such concern for a vine, how much more concern should there be for the lost of Nineveh, which number 120,000? Jonah serves as a living example to us of someone who wasn't ruled by the heart. God used Jonah regardless, but at the same time, He left us with a question: Will our hearts for the lost include our enemies? Will we demonstrate the compassion of Christ for others?

Christ taught the same lesson in the parable of the Prodigal Son. The son who was lost returns after squandering his inheritance and repents of his sins. The older son, who had remained and cared for his father and land, was angry that his father was rejoicing in the return of his lost son. The parable, in the way it is structured, ends with a silent question that the listeners of Jesus' time would have understood: What heart do you have for the lost?

Making It Practical

So how do we practically demonstrate kindness, love and sympathy in today's changing world? Jesus loved His disciples—and He loves us—despite our temperament and socioeconomic status. He gives us His time, energy, love, and power to do the same for others.

First, practice the disciplines of study, prayer, and the morning watch as you've never done before. This is what enables you to see people as Christ would see them: hurting, lost, in pain, and in great need of His love.

Second, periodically ask yourself the heart-check questions. Are you guarding your heart well? If not, what changes do you need to make to once more have the wellspring of life flowing deeply from you to others? Make those changes.

Third, walk the talk. The words attributed to St. Francis of Assisi apply: "Preach the gospel at all times. Use words if necessary." Do your best to extend love, kindness, and sympathy to others.

> "'One loving spirit,' says St. Augustine, 'sets another afire.' Every day God finds some whose hearts are right toward Him and through whom, therefore, He can show Himself strong and deliver His word."[2]   **JRM**

If we don't make every effort to rule by the heart—to treat others with love—then we are no longer a threat to this world. We become irrelevant. Like the priest and the Levite in the story of the Good Samaritan, we will walk past the injured man on a winter sidewalk in Chicago. And that is the antithesis of all that John R. Mott prayed for the world and for us when he wrote his fifteen lessons. One day, we will be a completed work in Christ Jesus— and only then will we love with a perfect love—and have a heart like His.

"I will give you a new heart and put a new spirit within you," says Ezekiel 36:26 (NKJV).

Until then, all we have to do is ask our Lord for help.

LESSON 2
IN REFLECTION
For Yourself

1. Some Christians aren't known for ruling by the heart in love, kindness, and sympathy. What actions by Christians have resulted in this?
2. Of the questions on guarding your heart, are you struggling with one now? List three things you can do to bring this question back into balance.
3. Who would Jesus use as an example of your neighbor if He were speaking to you?
4. Mother Teresa said, "If you judge people, you have no time to love them." List the name of someone you have judged and need to reaffirm the value of in order to love them.
5. What are specific steps you can take this week to rule by the heart—to demonstrate love, kindness, and sympathy?

For Group Discussion and Leadership

1. How does your organization preach the gospel without using words?
2. What do you consider to be the "heart" of your organization? Using the author's suggestions, how can you guard your organization's heart?
3. Who do you consider to be your organization's neighbors? How does your organization demonstrate love to those neighbors?
4. How do you encourage and promote a culture that rules by the heart?

3

Study Priorities

No man can do all the good to be done in the world.
We need to list and study our own priorities daily.

JRM

by Lori Swann

It was Monday morning in the office. In front of me was the neatly typed to-do list from my Sunday night ritual of planning out the week. The list covered two pages. It was color-coded by priority and impact. A woman in charge—that was me. With responsibilities both to one of the largest YMCAs in the country and to one of the largest branches in the association, I couldn't afford to waste time on little things.

Tap, tap.

The knock came on my glass door, and a feeling of despair hit my stomach as I saw the building supervisor tightly holding our resident troublemaker, David. "Not today," I moaned out loud. "Not again," I thought to myself.

David was twelve years old and a constant nuisance around the Y. He got into fights, broke things, and taunted the staff. At one point, we had brought in his parents with the intention of suspending his membership, but when we met his parents we just couldn't do it. They blamed the Y for not having enough things to keep David occupied and out of trouble. They were busy professionals. An older couple who had already raised other children, they considered David to be an unwanted surprise. So they dropped him off at the Y every day with a lunch and a ten-dollar bill. Most nights it was close to closing, and sometimes after, when they picked him up. The staff and I agreed that the Y was the best place for him and that we would do what we could to help him stay out of trouble.

I had said "we" would do everything we could, but what I really thought was "they" would take care of it. After all, my training was in business. They were the experts in children and the psychology and activities that were best suited for troubled kids, right? If not, why did I hire them?

So, the "not again" frustrations I was feeling were as targeted at the staff as they were at David. I had things to do. Things that really mattered. What would happen if I didn't finish my rolling-year-end? I couldn't imagine. I had reports to write, strategies to plan. People counted on me.

"Bring them to me." Huh? *"Bring them to me."* The phrase played over and over in my mind. And then I remembered. Jesus had made time for children. He had commanded the disciples to bring the children in Matthew 19:14. Jesus had the most important of things to do, and yet He still made children a priority.

My heart changed toward David and to other underloved children that day. I felt instant shame at my misaligned priorities. "Forgive me," I prayed, and without a doubt, He did. I also have no doubt that David was blessed by our work with him at the Y. I made him my personal assistant. He must have changed the letters on the marquee a thousand times over the next year. He didn't mature overnight, but years later he came by the Y and asked for me. I wasn't there, but he left a message to let me know how much he appreciated all the Y had done for him. He was about to graduate from college and credited the Y for teaching him about work and honor.

I've thought so many times about what might have happened if I had taken my self-important attitude and vented my frustrations at David. And my prayer became, "Thank you, Lord, for saving me from myself once again."

Too Much of a Good Thing?

"Study priorities." Mott implies it's not enough to set them, but that we should continually study them. He must have known, like our Father in heaven, that it wouldn't be as easy as making a to-do list. New opportunities would come at us daily that would attempt to move up on our list of priorities. The world tells us to put ourselves first: "Take care of you first, then others." Many of us came of age in the "me" generation. But even if you've decided the best way to live is not to put yourself first, what do you put first? If you were raised to say, and maybe even live, with God in first place, what comes next—work, school, church, hobbies, or family? All good things, but all easily deceive us into believing they need more of us.

Is there ever too much of a good thing? I was raised in a Christian home. My mom never missed a church service, be it Sunday morning, Sunday night, or Wednesday night. It was useless to even ask if you could stay home, even if you were sick. I remember once being left in the car with a fever while my mom played the piano for the service. She had important work to do! There was no one else who could possibly fill her shoes. Later in life when we talked about it, we laughed at her misaligned priorities. No blame was laid, but we both laughed at how easy it is to even let a good thing lead us astray.

Maybe you know families that have let their children occupy too many places on the priority list. As a mother of four and lover of children, that's hard for me to even write, but it can happen. Quality time with children is important, but more often, in its place, we focus on running our children to and from school and sports activities or buying them things we can't afford and they don't need to show them we love them. Americans have more personal debt than any other country. Stand in line at Wal-Mart and see people buying their children expensive toys that once would have been reserved only for Christmas or a birthday. Wander through Limited Too or Abercrombie and watch parents spending hundreds of dollars on clothes that children will outgrow after one season. What is the priority? Sometimes it's to fill a need that the adult never had as a child.

When I was a child, I lived in a house trailer. It was the source of a lot of shame and embarrassment for both me and my sister. We often said that when we were grown up, we would never live in trailers. Much of my drive in life is based on my upbringing; I never wanted to be poor or embarrassed again. I graduated first in my class, was the first in my family to finish college, and made more money than I ever thought I would. Still, I pushed myself to have more: more money, more security, more things for my kids.

The Influence of Others

I've noticed with all my children that when they go to kindergarten they begin to get some of their own priorities mixed up. When my son Mac went to kindergarten, he began to come home every day in want. He wanted a different backpack, different shoes, and different toys. My husband and I were both working more than fifty hours a week to provide what we thought was the best of everything. We lived in a nice house, drove nice cars, and dressed both Morgan, our oldest, and Mac in a way that would never embarrass them. Or so we thought.

Mac began to be obsessed with Charlie's house. "Why can't we have a house like Charlie's?" he would beg. "Man, Mom, I wish you could just see it," he would exclaim with a sigh. I became fed up with his constant wanting and told him so. "Mac," I said, "There will always be someone with a better house or car or clothes or toys. You have to learn to be satisfied with what God has given you." I preached a lesson I had yet to learn but was eager to pass on. So imagine my surprise one day when we drove through what I considered to be an eyesore of a trailer park in our community: Mac sat up straight and pointed, "Look Mom, there it is: Charlie's house. Isn't it wonderful? It has wheels on it, Mom, and when they move they just take it with them!"

In Proverbs 22:6, we're told that we are teaching our children in a way that they will never depart from. We often think of that in the positive, but the reverse is also true. When we as parents or role models for children don't have our priorities in order, what are we teaching? Thank goodness we can also learn from the children.

Soon after this lesson in priorities, my husband and I made a drastic change. We decided we just couldn't both keep working at the pace we were going and be everything that we wanted to be and that God and our children needed us to be. We decided, after much thought and prayer, that my husband, Kenny, would quit his job and stay home with the kids. He was the bigger wage earner, but his job in auto manufacturing left him tired and frustrated. I loved my job, so even though I made less, we couldn't see it happening the other way around.

Now this is a man who, until I married him, had never washed a dish, much less a load of clothes. He didn't make his own toast or fill up his own glass of tea, but he was willing to learn. And so we set off on one of our most wonderful and terrifying adventures so far in our twenty years together. We put our family first and never regretted doing so, even though our lifestyle changed drastically. Expensive vacations and eating out were a thing of the past. Ironically, after a visit to my aunt's house where the kids played in the yard with their cousins, we asked Morgan and Mac to compare it to a recent trip to Disney World, where we had flown to Orlando, visited all the parks, and spent thousands of dollars. They both preferred the visit to family, yet we had splurged on Disney because of the kids . . . or so we thought. Makes me think of Matthew 6:19–21:

> Do not lay up for yourselves treasures on earth, where moth and rust destroy and where thieves break in and steal; but lay up for yourselves treasures in heaven, where neither moth nor rust destroys and where thieves do not break in and steal. For where your treasure is, there your heart will be also. (NKJV)

The Bottom Line

Over and over the Bible makes it clear that we are not to be just about making money in this world, both in written verse as above, and also in the way Jesus lived. Our American culture makes this advice especially hard to follow. It's just easier to live when you have enough of everything. And it isn't just families or individuals that get caught up in keeping score of their lives with their bank accounts. Good community organizations do it, too.

Many churches today feel they need big, lavish buildings to attract people. YMCAs abandon storefronts to move to huge facilities with every recreation and fitness offering. Corporate offices of nonprofits, Scouts, United Ways, and Boys and Girls Clubs often are indiscernible from their for-profit counterparts. What is the priority?

I have the opportunity to work with many Ys. Some have only one scorecard: the bottom line. Some will even acknowledge this, apologize, and then move quickly to the true but misleading, "There's no mission without money." But how much money should a church or a community service organization have? Many have millions in reserves in the name of safety and security.

The problem lies not in having or measuring money; it's with having only one scorecard that causes us to make decisions that get our priorities out of line. Take the family that needs something, be it a bigger house, car, better vacation, more money in the bank—before they can enjoy life. Time goes by. Mom and Dad work hard to make all their dreams come true. Either they are never home to spend time teaching and loving their children, or when they are home, they are so focused on things and money that they take all the joy out of living. God wants us to have joy in our lives, and He tells us there's no way to have that unless we put Him first, not money.

Organizations that put money first are incapable of ministering to their members in an effective way. I have an MBA so no one loves a good ratio more than me, but money should be one criterion, not the only indicator of whether we're doing a good job. If it were that easy, if it were just about how much money was in the bank, or how efficiently we could operate, anyone could make leadership decisions. It's when we're asked to balance the lives of people with the financial health of the organization that we need God's wisdom.

Several years ago, I found a homeless family on the street outside my downtown office. They had two young children and another on the way. I reached out to help, and in my usual single-minded way, expected everyone else to do so, too. I gave my own funds and raised others to help this family get out of the shelter and into an apartment. I pleaded with and bullied social service agencies until they had food, shelter, and health care. I was so impassioned by their plight that I went to my church and asked what they could do. I thought they would be as excited as I was about the potential to make a difference in this family. But the church said they couldn't give because this family was out of their service area. *"Out of their service area?"* I missed that part of the Bible where it said go to the four corners of your service area and, well, you know the rest.

In a bad case of timing, the church's Wednesday evening business meeting included an agenda item for the approval of a new ten-thousand-dollar piano. A ten-thousand-dollar piano! I love music and even play the piano, but I thought they had to be kidding me. We definitely had different priorities. I sarcastically asked if I could have the box the piano came in. Maybe the family could live there? It was a life-changing moment for me—the moment I realized that the church in which I had grown up couldn't be trusted to take my tithes and offerings and spend them in a way that I felt God had led my priorities.

> **"No man can do: (a) all the good that needs to be done;** (b) all that others want him to do; (c) all that he himself wants to do. Therefore, he must acquire the habit of putting first things first. . . . Each day we should be asking, What does Christ want me to be and do today?"[1]
>
> **JRM**

To be fair, I realize that the church probably did have to have some kind of rules about giving. And maybe they needed that piano. But for me, people who were hungry and without shelter would always have to come first in my giving and sharing decisions. That's what I knew God was leading me to.

Investing Our Treasures

When Mott tells us to "study priorities," he is telling us to constantly assess what will give us the best return on our investment of time or treasure. There's more to be done than we can do, but God will lead each of us to where our treasure is best invested. For some of us, it will be children. For others, it will be seniors, teens, or adults. If we all had the same group as our priority, many needs would go unmet. So while we know that God wants us to put Him first, others second, and ourselves third, it may be that you will need to study who it is that the others are for you. What are the gifts God gave you and how can you align your priorities for others with those gifts?

"Relationship" is the buzzword in organizations today. For-profit and not-for-profit businesses alike know that by building relationships with their stakeholders, the job of retaining customers and members is easier. If attrition goes down, profitability goes up. Many spend time training their staff on the best way to build relationships through getting to know people, finding ways to use their gifts to God's glory, and to involve them in the organization. "Love your neighbor as yourself," is how the Bible tells us to build relationships. Just by loving people—our neighbors, our coworkers, our board members, our constituents, our world—we can build relationships and improve our organizations and ourselves.

Mott also told us to list our priorities. I still enjoy my Sunday night ritual of making my to-do list for the week to come, just like I did when I was fortunate enough to cross paths with David many years ago. For most of us, until we write it down, it just won't get done. My teenagers are taught in high school to keep assignment lists. It's the American way.

> "In any work abounding in pressing needs and great opportunities, we must make a study of priorities. We must plan the use of our time."[2]   **JRM**

Today our to-do lists are often kept in elaborate and sometimes expensive planners. Sometimes they are filed electronically for our coworkers and clients to see. I once heard a Christian talk show host say if he could look at a person's weekly planner, he could tell whether that person was happy without ever having met them. It's true, though. I've heard the same thing said about a bank statement. Just like Matthew 6:21 says, you can sure tell a lot about where our heart lies from where we spend our time and money. Sometimes we might think we just haven't had time to set priorities yet, but that's a fallacy. By having none, it is never ourselves that get neglected, but others. Human nature requires us to make a conscious choice every day to put God and others first in our lives.

There's so much good to be done. Instead of becoming overwhelmed by the task, be deliberate as you list your priorities this week: God first, others second, self last. When you put God first, everything else will just fall into place.

LESSON 3
IN REFLECTION
For Yourself

1. List what you believe Jesus' top three priorities were.
2. What actions did Jesus take to keep these priorities front and center?
3. What actions can you take to keep your priorities front and center?
4. Where is your time and treasure best invested according to God's purpose?

For Group Discussion and Leadership

1. What are your organization's priorities?
2. How does sound fiscal management interact with these priorities? How do you ensure that fiscal management doesn't override the core of your organization?
3. What will give your organization the best return on investment of time and treasure?

4

We Can Trust Others

We can afford great acts of trust.
I can testify that I have never
had others disappoint me.
JRM

by Eric Ellsworth

I could just tell he was a tough, old farmer. He wore overalls, and it looked like he'd come straight from the field. As for me, I must've been close to forty, and I was making my way off the stage at a gospel sing. Back then, I played Christian music and toured an area that covered a couple of states.

He walked right up to me and said, "Are you Jack Ellsworth's son?" I said no, that Jack was actually my grandfather, and right there in front of me, the man started to cry.

He told me a story about growing up in the Depression, when his parents would send him to my grandfather's dairy to pick up some milk. Nobody really had any money back then, but when my grandfather slid the milk across the counter to the boy, he'd slide the boy's nickel back to him, as well. Even after all those years, that act of kindness still brought tears to his eyes. He wept.

By then, my grandfather had long passed away. But the encounter brought me new insight into the kind of man he was. He was someone who regularly put others before himself, someone who really believed the best about people—and chances are, someone who was so humble that he wouldn't have allowed himself to be disappointed by another. He and John R. Mott probably would have gotten along quite well.

The first time I heard that Mott said he'd never had others disappoint him, I admit I was surprised. I thought of the many times in my own life that people had disappointed me. Then, I had a revelation: if we learn to love people unconditionally, the way that Christ loves us, then there's no way those people can let us down. We will want only the best for them. And, as Mott puts it, we'll be able to afford great acts of trust.

So What Is Trust, Anyway?

Webster's dictionary describes trust as "confidence in a person or a thing, because of the qualities one perceives." It is also described as an "acceptance of something as true," and as "a faith in the future."

Now, growing up, I seemed to have my share of disappointment. Though I would say I was very blessed as a young boy, I remember, for example, the disappointment that came when I never received a pony that had been promised for my birthday. But the disappointment passed, thanks to the innocence and purity in my childhood heart. That could be another reason Jesus said we must "be like little children" in order to be accepted into His kingdom. Children are quick to forgive, quick to forget, and unjaded by the wrongs of this world.

As we grow, though, trust becomes the basis of all relationships. Think of a marriage. In its purest form, it's two people who entrust their spirits, minds, and bodies; their resources; their futures; and their whole selves to each other. Any breach of that trust is destructive and has terrible consequences. All relationships which are based in trust either remain healthy or are harmed based on trust fulfilled or unfulfilled.

The way I see it, trust is built through doing what you say you will do, when you say you'll do it, and the way you said it would be done. When I think of my work in the YMCA and of the employees who do what they say they will do, the "trust bank account" increases with every positive installment. If we are trustworthy as employees, we are those who keep our promises. We do not overpromise nor underdeliver. This inspires the confidence of those to whom we are responsible and of the people we serve. Trust is built or broken based on what we do or do not do.

As Christians, though, we have an added tool in our toolbox when it comes to trusting others. If we are prayerful in all things as the Scriptures implore us, we will be able to discern through the Holy Spirit whom we should trust and to what degree. I have an idea that Mott, through his life of prayer and service, walked so closely with God that he knew whom to trust—and as such, how to extend enough grace that he would not be disappointed.

Trusting God First

I've noticed it in my own life: The closer I walk with Christ, the less my disappointment level in other people. It's because I become more and more confident that His will is going to be done, and that I can trust others because I have checked with Him in advance through prayer.

My greatest disappointments, and perhaps even my only disappointments, have come when I am far from fellowship with God or when I did not trust Him enough to obediently follow His instructions.

Christians are taught that we can trust God. Proverbs 3:5–6 says: "Trust in the Lord with all your heart; and lean not on your own understanding" (NKJV). 1 Peter 5:7 tells us, "Cast all your anxieties on him; because he cares for you" (NRSV). With all of these assurances that God will produce good for His people, we can afford great acts of confidence and trust in others.

Now, I would never suggest that we blindly trust others. If we lead an organization and someone comes up to us and asks us to give ten thousand dollars and to trust them to do something good with it, it would be foolish to do so. (It might be more prudent to take off running!) But if we were to build a relationship with that person and learn and discern what the cause and effect might be of making this investment, we may find it to be a trustworthy request. Before we arrived at that point, though, we'd need a little optimism.

I wonder how much of Mott's statement about *never* having been disappointed has to do with positive thinking and his nearly infinite optimism about the outcomes for which he strived. It's my understanding that in his fund-raising efforts during the war years, he gathered more than a quarter of a billion dollars for war relief efforts. If this were translated into today's dollars, it would make Mott the most prolific fund-raiser in the history of the YMCA movement and perhaps in nonprofit history. It is impossible to make this kind of impact without a giant portion of optimism and positive thinking. Of course, it takes more than optimism to get great results. But, optimism that comes as a result of abiding and trusting in God, is sure to bring great results "pressed down, shaken together, and running over" (Luke 6:38 NKJV).

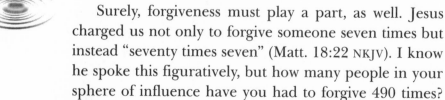

"When we have committed definite responsibility to a man, we should trust him with it. . . . Men respond to trust. They rise to great heights when faith is manifested in them."[1]   JRM

Surely, forgiveness must play a part, as well. Jesus charged us not only to forgive someone seven times but instead "seventy times seven" (Matt. 18:22 NKJV). I know he spoke this figuratively, but how many people in your sphere of influence have you had to forgive 490 times? That's a lot of forgiveness! I think Jesus' point is that with real forgiveness, it is as if the wrong never happened. If we forgive the way Jesus forgave, the wrong is completely forgotten and trust is instantly restored.

In practical application, I think about employees who could be seen as disappointments. Perhaps they don't achieve the predetermined goals that we have set together, and our confidence erodes in trusting that they will accomplish the desired results. This is indeed a difficult situation. But with true forgiveness, we may be disappointed in the outcome, but not the person. It may seem like splitting hairs, but I believe it's the secret to maintaining relationships and moving forward to better results.

Not Going It Alone

As YMCA leaders, we work toward making an impact in our communities. It's a huge undertaking, and there is no way for us to do it alone. When I think of trying to take on my responsibilities without others to assist me, it's clearly impossible. In a sense, then, we simply *must* afford great acts of trust. We have no other choice, for it is the only way the work can be accomplished.

I think of our annual fund-raising campaign and the small army we put together to raise the money on an annual basis. If it were not for this pyramid of leaders devoting themselves to the task of serving others, it wouldn't happen. Mott apparently understood this, as well. Even though he was able to single-handedly raise large sums of money to further the distinctly Christian work of the YMCA, he was clearly dependent on a legion of fund-raisers and donors to make his vision a reality.

Jesus, too, was surrounded by others, and I have to wonder if He would claim that anyone had ever disappointed him. When Judas stepped forward and kissed Jesus on the cheek, what was going through His mind? Certainly, Judas betrayed Jesus' trust, but was He disappointed that Judas did it? I don't think so. He knew that

Judas was doing what had to be done, and that His death was preordained.

Was Jesus disappointed in the woman at the well, the disciples arguing over who would be greater in the kingdom, the money changers in the temple, or the Pharisees whom he called "hypocrites"? Sure, Jesus displayed emotion in these situations, but I believe He understood the sinful nature of man so well, and loved us so much, that disappointment melted into compassion and love. Just the thought of Jesus giving His life for a people so depraved should be enough to humble even the most self-absorbed of us.

Lessons For Us

Of course, all this talk of trust can have great application as we strive to put Christian principles into practice in our daily lives. As we walk closely with God and see other people through His eyes, we can afford those great acts of trust. We can afford great acts of trust in staff. We can afford great acts of trust in volunteers. We can afford great acts of trust in each other.

> **"Once let a man become convinced that God has a plan** and a definite work for him, and that no other man can perform it, and you introduce into his life a motive and a motivating power which will enable him to transcend his handicaps and limitations and will carry him through all opposition."[2]   **JRM**

We need each other to accomplish the things which God desires of us; so really, there's no place for disappointment or mistrust. It only takes away time and energy. Philippians 4:8 says, ". . . whatever is true, whatever is honorable, whatever is just, whatever is pure, whatever is pleasing, whatever is commendable, if there is any excellence and if there is anything worthy of praise, think about such things" (NRSV). If we are absorbed in the pure and the lovely, there will be little time for anything else.

The Challenge Ahead

Even after all this time, my grandfather remains my number-one role model. That's mostly because he was so gentle and kind, but it is also because he was the kind of person who inspired trust. He always showed me that I could believe the best about him through his faithfulness. If you want to be a positive role model, practice faithfulness. You'll be amazed at the trust you will receive. My grandfather was a man like John R. Mott, whose life spoke volumes and whose faithfulness inspired the trust of a multitude of people.

My guess is that Mott, in talking about trust and disappointment, knew that his statement would challenge others to their very core. He must have known that through a lack of trust, wars would start, families would be destroyed, and friendships would be lost forever. It's up to us, then, to be the salt and light that make a difference, extending to others what the world won't. It's up to us to put others first, to humbly walk with God, and to trust.

LESSON 4
IN REFLECTION

For Yourself

1. How would you define trust? How would Jesus define trust?
2. How has God taught you to trust Him?
3. Think of a time when you were greatly disappointed. Was your relationship with God close or distant when this happened? What would have been different in how you handled that disappointment if you'd felt closer to God at the time?
4. Can you choose to not be disappointed in others? How or how not?

For Group Discussion and Leadership

1. The world often teaches us not to trust others. How does your organization encourage staff and volunteers to trust each other?
2. What role does leadership in an organization play in establishing trust?
3. Trust is a key component in building an effective team. Share examples of ways Jesus built trust with his disciples.
4. What steps will you take as a leader to encourage great acts of trust?

5

Study and Promote the Use of the Bible

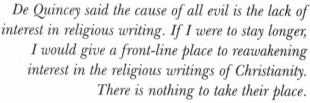

De Quincey said the cause of all evil is the lack of interest in religious writing. If I were to stay longer, I would give a front-line place to reawakening interest in the religious writings of Christianity. There is nothing to take their place.

JRM

by Jay W. Lippy

In that one moment, it all became clear.

I was barely twenty, married for only six months, and my new wife had been pregnant for two of them. I was sitting on the edge of my bed with a deep fear coursing through my veins because I had no idea what would come next. The truth was I had no idea how to be a man, much less a father.

I had grown up without a father of my own. He died when I was four, and my stepfather—well, we certainly had our differences. But this young woman, this pastor's daughter who had caught my eye, was counting on me. My dilemma was how to be something I had never seen or experienced.

I remember so clearly sitting there, almost numb, as it all began to sink in. But in that panic-filled moment, I also remembered the comfort of the Word and the knowledge it offered. If I would be faithful to follow God, I knew deep down that He would be the Daddy I never had and He would teach me everything I needed to know. He promised to send me truth and comfort, and He did—through the Bible. It truly became a consistent guide for my life.

When I'm asked a question like, "Why should I read the Bible?" my first thought is to give a discourse about its authenticity, to try and prove that it really is the sovereign Word of God. More about that a little later.

> **"If you abide in the Word—that is, if you spend time** there, if you dwell there, if you live there—then you will necessarily be a true disciple. Such Bible study alone shows us the needs of our spiritual lives. It reveals to us the weak places in our armor, the points of least resistance in our lives. It shows us ourselves as we are, and therefore as God sees us."[1]   **JRM**

It must be said that for centuries untold numbers have cited the Bible as their major source of personal strength, encouragement, wisdom, guidance, and knowledge. Without a doubt, it has been all of that and more for me. I'm now a husband of twenty-seven years, father of three adult children, and grandfather of two grandsons. In all these years of experience, that day sitting on the edge of my bed would be just one of countless occasions when fear gripped my heart, understanding left my mind, and my character waned under stress or temptation. But, God's Word always came through. My heavenly Father, through the Scriptures, has taught me how to be a man, how to be a husband, and how to be a father. Time and again, He has revealed truth to my heart simply because I spent time alone with Him in prayer and in His Word. I'm forever grateful for His mercy, His far-reaching grace, and His never-ending guidance marvelously revealed though the written Word.

Bringing the Bible to Bear

I don't profess to be a biblical scholar, but after more than a quarter century of reading, preaching, counseling, and experiencing personally those things found within its pages, I ardently hold that there is more than plausibility for accepting the authenticity of the Bible, the claims of God as sovereign, the personage of Jesus Christ and His sacrificial death on the cross, and the influence, sealing, leading and freedom found through the Holy Spirit. We need not hide, however, the simple reality that faith is the key component in the Christian life. Romans 10:17 says, "So then, faith comes by hearing, and hearing by the Word of God" (NKJV).

John R. Mott understood this when he suggested we "bring the Bible to bear upon all problems," and that "all evils are due to not living in accordance with Scriptures."

I wasn't fortunate enough to walk with Mott and see how this played out in his daily life, but I was blessed to have a friend who saw things from the same perspective. He modeled this idea of "bringing the Bible to bear" before my very eyes.

> **"To do the work of God we must have the power of God.** To have the power of God we must have the Spirit of God. The Bible is the channel through which the Spirit comes into the life. . . . If we would be filled with the Spirit, keep filled and have our capacity constantly increase, let us become possessed with the Bible-study passion."[2] **JRM**

With difficult circumstances at home, I became a troubled teenager. I quit high school as a freshman and failed three times getting there. I'll never forget what my high school counselor said to me on the day I left school: "You're a loser, you will always be a loser, and I'm glad to see you leave this school." Thank God my friend Noah did not see things the same way.

Noah was my roommate in the navy and was the first Christian I had ever met. He didn't quote Scripture every time he opened his mouth, but he studied the Bible. He was a man who truly believed the Bible, and as a result his life modeled what he read. He literally loved me to Christ. So, through his example, when I needed somewhere to turn, I knew exactly where to go: the Living and active Word of God. I saw that the Bible was God's personal love letter to me.

Of course, understanding that point took some faith. While there is an abundance of historical, archaeological, scientific, and prophetic "proofs" that give support to biblical claims, faith still plays a major role in accepting what God has to say in His Word. Here is an example: it takes faith to explain that romantic love exists. As a couple enters into marriage, they must accept by faith that their intended really loves them. It is scientifically impossible to prove love's existence beyond a shadow of a doubt; yet through tender acts of kindness and years of being in an intimate relationship, couples testify to love's thrill, endurance, and steadfast impact upon their lives. God's touch is felt with no less certainty and with no less tangible impact.

And It Still Applies

It takes faith not only to believe that the Word of God is true but that it also includes wisdom applicable today—a wisdom that can affect our own lives as well as the lives of those around us.

Faith-based organizations, for example, can benefit greatly from posting Scriptures and hosting Bible studies that help others dive into the Word. I know the idea makes some business-minded people uncomfortable, but as I see it, we don't have to be all things to all people. Before becoming a chaplain, I was a YMCA senior program director for many years. Along the way, I noticed something interesting. I'm an avid basketball fan, but I discovered that when we talked about basketball events or posted flyers about our leagues, the racquetball crowd didn't seem to mind, nor was it offended. And when the fitness center advertised marathons or body building classes, the gymnasts didn't rise up in arms. So when we started Bible studies, we posted flyers. We wanted to be gracious, kind, and open about our intentions to study the Bible. We were up-front and honest, "This will be a Bible study. If you want to come, great, and if you do not, that is fine, too." Amazingly, no one was offended. I discovered that having such a presence in the branch brought hope and unity; those who were involved really grew in their faith and many who didn't attend were glad that we held the study.

On a personal level, when dealing with staff who don't know Christ as their Savior, I find myself teaching biblical principles through the things they do every day at the YMCA. If someone is kind, benevolent, or caring, for example, I'll use a scriptural example, and ask, "Did you know what you are doing is a very biblical thing?" It's a great opportunity to show how the Bible and biblical concepts are tangible so people can see that this "God thing" is not taboo.

> **"Would we be Christians of more than ordinary** spiritual power? Then we must be great feeders upon the Word, which is not only quick but powerful."[3]　**JRM**

I've met many Christians over the years who've been a little timid about delving into serious Bible study, as well as those who consider it a chore. If the problem is a lack of understanding, concordances and Bible software can be a great help. These resources offer clarification and can supplement regular Bible reading with fun and interesting facts.

In life, there are some things we do that we don't have a passion for but we do them anyway because they are the right thing to do. In marriage, for example, there are some things I just don't like to do . . . mostly because I'm selfish. When you are in a relationship with someone you love, however, you willingly make sacrifices. After time, you fall so in love with that person that the challenge of doing those things which you dislike pale in comparison. Once you get your "self" out of the way, you begin to see the benefits and often your attitude toward the task changes and it actually becomes something enjoyable.

At first, it takes a little discipline. Sometimes people have a false idea that doing a Bible study means you must read dozens of chapters daily or something similar. But, it may be that you examine only a few verses and prayerfully consider them throughout the day. Studying the Bible is not so much about the number of chapters you read as it is spending time with God and developing an intimate closeness with Him. It is in that relationship where God reveals Himself to you. Bible study is fruitful but should never take the place of spending time with Him. It may start out as a duty, something you feel you have to do, but eventually it becomes a treasure as it brings you great hope.

Good Works

I believe most Christians understand that it's part of our responsibility to do good works. One of the problems I observe, however, is that we take our cue from men rather than prayerfully considering what God would have us do. In the days of Jesus, the Pharisees were legalistic in their rules and regulations on how to be faithful. They certainly were not kind or loving, and grace never entered their unobtainable goals. The ultimate end of their teaching was bondage and guilt because no one could possibly live up to their more than 613 laws. Today many people, like the Pharisees, are busy doing religious deeds, but just because they are working hard does not mean they are pleasing God.

In Ephesians 2:10, the apostle Paul says we are created to do good works because we are God's workmanship. Could anything be more clear? We must do good works. *Wait . . . rewind.* Is this passage telling us that we must do more? No. I believe that Christ wants us to know that we already *are* His good work. Therefore, by being Bible students, we learn that being in a relationship *with* God is more important than doing good works *for* God.

Again, one of the ways to reflect Him to the world is to fall in love with Him through His Word. When we focus on knowing Christ, when we take time to study the Bible, when we fellowship with other followers of Christ and see them as our brothers and sisters, we then testify to the world that God loves them, too.

Of course, there will always be doubters, and there will always be those who question the usefulness and authenticity of God's Word. I promised earlier that we would talk more about that, so here it goes.

First, it's important to remember that the Bible doesn't claim to be a science book, even though it remains scientifically accurate. Nor does it claim to be an historical or archaeological book of facts, yet it remains sound on both accounts. Don't be afraid to put the Bible to question; your findings may in fact lay to rest those very things which prohibit you from fully trusting in God. If you've never seriously questioned your faith, then perhaps your faith is questionable.

The Bible contends that it was authored by God (2 Timothy 3:16). While not violating the personality of the individual human writers, He used the hands of peasants and kings, slaves and freemen, rich and poor—forty different authors—over the span of fifteen hundred years. It remains seamless in content and consistent in topic. Inside its pages, you will find information on subjects from finances to government; romance to community service; passionate sex to personal accountability; and business practices to parenting skills. As such, it's no wonder the Bible is a timeless source for virtually every aspect of life, death, and the promise of life ever after. It is true that recent times have ushered in numerous modern translations, but they come from the same original Greek and

Hebrew texts. From the eyewitness accounts of the apostles to the commentary of saints through the ages, I know of no other source of writings which has had such a lasting and profound impact upon humanity. In my estimation, that is because the Bible truly is what it claims to be—the unadulterated Word of God. For centuries, the Bible has withstood the constant criticism of skeptics, endured the continuous unfounded claims of doubters, and perhaps most important, withstood the test of time. Modern science is afforded the luxury of continuously updating itself to correct previously proclaimed "facts," but the Bible has remained unchanged and in no need of revision.

> **"It is that Bible study which will make us better men** tomorrow than today; . . . which enables us to meet God and to hear His voice and to know that it is His voice. It is that Bible study which opens up to us, each day, further and further vistas into the possibilities of the life hid with Christ in God."[4]   **JRM**

So, even today, when you open the pages of the Bible, and with an open heart ask God to reveal truth to you, He will. Your own honest research and heartfelt prayer will bring to light those truths that only faith can make real.

Little Reminders

For me, as a Christian, deep Bible study has changed my once reckless life into one that is grounded in grace—in His unmerited favor—and set it toward being free from the bondage that once held me back. In turn, that has allowed me to risk being who God has created me to be rather than struggling uselessly to measure up to standards I could never meet through my own effort.

Once in awhile, God gives me a reminder that, just as He promised all those years ago, He will use His Word to lead me if only I'm willing to follow.

It happened again recently when I returned to Pennsylvania to bury my best friend. He was only forty-two. We were thirteen when we started drinking together, and it was absolute liver failure that ended his life. It was literally a sobering experience to go back to preside over his funeral and to look into the eyes of childhood friends I had not seen in twenty-five years. Oh, what my life might have been if I, like my friend, had believed that I was in control. What if I had not accepted the power and direction that has always been available to me through the Bible? What if I had done my own thing?

Jesus didn't do His "own thing." He allowed God to direct His every step, and the result was perfection. How awesome it would be if we stopped working so hard to do things for God and focused instead on spending our time with Him, allowing Him to write into our lives on a daily basis the things He wants us to be. I suggest that being is a lot harder than doing. If we choose to direct our own lives and how we will live out this Christian life, we will ultimately end up setting God aside. Understanding His Word is essential. It's the instruction manual for daily living—not to mention a personal love letter that God has written to each of us. Why not spend some time with Him and find out what He has in store for you!

LESSON 5
IN REFLECTION
For Yourself

1. Define faith. Hebrews 11:1 says, "Now faith is the substance of things hoped for, the evidence of things not seen" (NKJV). How is faith the key?
2. The New Testament was written by eyewitnesses to Jesus' life. How does that fact affect your faith?
3. What does God want you to do regarding His Word?
4. Describe a time in your life when the Bible provided wisdom and counsel in a difficult situation or when you wished for sound spiritual guidance in a time of need.

For Group Discussion and Leadership

1. Discuss how your organization can use the Bible as a major source of:
    - personal strength for organizational leaders
    - encouragement in difficult times
    - wisdom when making critical decisions
    - guidance when dealing with others
    - knowledge when planning
    - a visible and public part of your organization's foundation.

    Identify a Bible verse for each of the above items of discussion.
2. List two or three principles from the Bible that govern your choices as an organization, e.g. let us behave decently (Rom. 13:13).

6

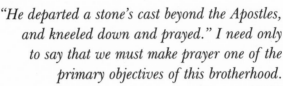

The Discipline of Prayer
Is Essential

"He departed a stone's cast beyond the Apostles,
and kneeled down and prayed." I need only
to say that we must make prayer one of the
primary objectives of this brotherhood.
JRM

by Sean Allison

I have never initiated a single prayer I've ever prayed.

Not the ones screamed from beneath the stars, asking God for intervention in my teen years. Not the ones whispered in the stillness of night, claiming healing for my son with Down's syndrome. Not even the ones spoken through tears, when I'd reached the end of my rope and needed a new start.

No, God was the one reaching out to me, always there, waiting for me to respond to Him about the things I was experiencing. He was the one, all along, who was teaching me that life without prayer is like life without oxygen.

I'm always surprised when I hear people say they don't want to bother God with their requests. Too often, we think of Him as someone doing something else, yet a phone call away, ready to answer whenever we call. But, I don't think that's accurate. The truth is, He never hung up from our last conversation, and is simply there, waiting for our voice.

Somehow, I think this is something John R. Mott understood. In discussing lessons learned from a lifetime of YMCA service, Mott encouraged us to make prayer

51

"one of the primary objectives" of the brotherhood. He wrote and spoke extensively on the subject of prayer, and saw clearly how prayer could win the world for Christ. You might even say he was obsessed with prayer. And that's a great example to follow.

Missing God's Heart

Prayer is a tool God gave us to build a relationship with Him. It was given to us to move our hearts in line with His, and to make His plans for our lives a reality. Unfortunately, there are many misconceptions about how that happens. I think most people will agree that God exists, and that prayer is a way to be connected with Him. But, sometimes we can institutionalize it, turning it into a rote practice. We want to make sure we put prayer on the agenda as one of the bases to be covered, or one of the t's that needs to be crossed. If we're getting together for a meeting, or about to travel on a trip, or having a meal together, that's the place for prayer. I'm not saying that's bad at all. But, I am saying it's bad if that's 90 percent of our prayer life. If it is, we've completely missed God's heart, as well as the intimacy He wants us to enjoy and experience through communicating with Him.

It Begins with Jesus

All relationships have a starting point. And with God, it begins with Jesus. As Mott put it, He is the foundation. In John 14:6, Jesus tells us, "I am the way, the truth and the life, no man cometh unto the Father, but by me" (KJV). He died for our sins, was buried, and then rose and lives today. And our response to that is to pray, to put our faith in Jesus as Savior and Lord, ask God to forgive us of our sins, and invite Him into our lives. This is called the prayer of faith, and the result is the free gift of eternal life, which God provides by grace.

Our relationship with God then begins to grow, and out of gratitude for salvation, compelled by His Spirit, we pray and study Scripture which, according to

2 Timothy 3:16–17, was "given by inspiration of God, and is profitable for doctrine, for reproof, for correction, for instruction in righteousness, that the man of God may be complete, thoroughly equipped for every good work" (NKJV). And, as we continue in prayer and study, God reveals to us that He has a plan for our lives.

Now, God's plan can radically differ from what we might have planned on our own. Mott experienced this dilemma himself as a twenty-year-old college student at Cornell University. He wrote his parents, that even though he had intended to devote his energies to the legal profession and the service of his country, there had been "a constantly increasing impulse" urging him to devote his whole life and talents to the service of Jesus. "I at first warded off this prompting," he wrote, "but it gave me no rest and so for several weeks past I gave up and determined to see where the Spirit would impel me."

Mott is far from alone in his being "called." God calls all of us to serve Him in specific ways, according to the individual plan He has for our lives. Ephesians 2:10 says, "For we are His workmanship, created in Christ Jesus for good works, which God prepared beforehand that we should walk in them" (NKJV). Like all of us should, Mott kept in communication with God to find out what would happen next.

He Listens, He Hears

As our relationship with God grows, prayer enables it to remain personal and intimate and helps us stay on the right path. God is a living God, and His Spirit is alive within us. So it follows that we are able to sense His presence as He uses our conscience and the Scriptures to instruct and guide us.

In my own life, I can't think of a time in which prayer has not made a significant difference. Ever since I was ten years old and I prayed to receive Jesus into my heart, I have known that He was there. And I've known that, just as He has promised me, He will lead me beside the still waters, He will discipline me, and He will protect me. So, my prayer life is an ongoing conversation from the moment I rise, sometimes punctuated by focused intercession. I never feel like I'm out of earshot of the Lord. There's an old church saying that "where God guides He provides," and I've seen it in my own life over and over again. 1 John 5:14–15 reads, "Now this is the confidence that we have in Him, that if we ask anything according to His will, He hears us. And if we know that He hears us, whatever we ask, we know that we have the petitions that we have asked of Him" (NKJV).

Spreading the Gospel Through Prayer

In the summer of 1886, Mott served as Cornell's delegate to the first International Student Assembly in Mount Herman, Massachusetts. It was a conference, as Mott described it, in which, "Day after day in the long open spaces, the students in little groups went up into the foothills of the Green and White Mountains for intimate discussions and intercession." And it was, in his opinion, "the most significant Christian student conference ever held."

The results were amazing. A movement was launched that recruited, trained, and sent more than eighteen thousand student volunteers into the mission field around the world by 1944. The gospel was delivered to millions—without jet planes, e-mail, cell phones, overnight shipping, or the Internet. Just think about it: between now and 2055, if we were able to recruit, train, and place 360 people a year into the mission field, it would be powerful. God didn't need a satellite uplink to accomplish His plan back then, nor does He necessarily need one now. God's work simply requires praying people willing to follow His plan for their lives. Jesus said to His disciples, "whatever things you ask when you pray, believe that you receive them, and you will have them" (Mark 11:24 NKJV).

A life serving the Lord cannot be undertaken without prayer. The essence of prayer is to bring us into close fellowship with God and to keep us there until we meet Him face to face in eternity. In Mott's case, God put him on a path to become an evangelist and lead the YMCA Student Movement. The work God calls us to do may lead us to become an evangelist, teacher, or administrator, but the beginning and end of the journey is the same for us all. We start with Jesus, and our final destination is eternity with God—and prayer links the two together.

The Discipline of Prayer

Maybe we neglect it because it's so simple, but very few of us take full advantage of all that prayer has to offer. Our relationship with God has many valuable components, including studying, church activities, taking part in small groups, and listening to teaching or worship CDs. All have value and help our relationship with God, but none have quite the impact as prayer. We don't need to get dressed up to do it, it doesn't cost anything, and we can do it anywhere, but we still don't do it enough.

Prayer is the most powerful tool we have as Christians. Mott saw firsthand how prayer could change the world, and if we could catch that vision, the world would truly be a different place.

> **"Let us, in arranging our work for the year, plan for** intercessory prayer . . . This is the work most needed in the world. It is also the most Christlike work."[1]   **JRM**

That's true on a corporate level as well as an individual one. It's possible for organizations—such as the YMCA—to be known as Christian establishments led by prayer, but that can only happen if the people at the top are committed to the idea. Granted, any person in an organization can impact his or her own life and the lives of the people around them through building a relationship with Jesus Christ. But, when a group commits to prayer from the top down, it's not just an environment that can be changed. It's an entire culture, community, and world.

Think what could happen in organizations that offer a Monday morning devotional to start the week off right, allowing different people to lead and everyone to participate. Imagine praying together as a staff when challenges arise or goals are set. The results would be phenomenal.

So How Do We Do It?

All that we need to learn about prayer we can learn from Jesus' example and teaching. On a personal level, He instructed us to pray in private, underscoring the intimacy of our prayer relationship with God. Jesus taught in Matthew 6:6, "When you pray, go into your room, and when you have shut your door, pray to your Father who is in the secret place; and your Father who sees in secret will reward you openly" (NKJV). Often, He would separate Himself and spend time with His heavenly Father. Mott made note of this, quoting Luke 22:41: "And he [Jesus] was withdrawn from them about a stone's cast, and kneeled down, and prayed" (KJV). If Jesus—God, Savior, and Lord—found it profitable to spend time in prayer, why is it so hard for us?

> **"It is impossible to be consciously abiding in Christ** without real and frequent secret communion. In a word, secret prayer is prayer at its best."[2]   **JRM**

It could be because we're not exactly sure how to do it. Matthew 6:9–13 is called the Lord's Prayer. The disciples asked Jesus to teach them to pray, and He gave them and us a prayer template or outline to follow. Because in Matthew 6:7 He cautioned against prayers of "vain repetition," I believe the Lord's Prayer is not to be used in a systematic way every time we pray. There is nothing wrong with quoting it verbatim before God, but personalizing its different components creates a rich heartfelt expression to God. I see six basic elements in the prayer which are easy for us to adapt to our own circumstances.

1. Proper approach and address of God, since we're speaking to the most high, holy God, Creator of the universe and all things. "Our Father in heaven, hallowed be Your name."

2. Proper context, as we approach God to join Him in His work. Prayer is our response to Him. It is about His kingdom and His will. "Your Kingdom come, Your will be done on earth as it is in heaven."

3. Petition for any need in our lives, not just food. "Give us this day our daily bread."

4. Right forgiveness. When we come to a holy and righteous God who extends grace and mercy to us, eager to forgive us of our sins, we cannot stand before Him and hold any unforgiveness in our hearts toward any other person. "Forgive us our debts as we forgive our debtors."

5. A personal relationship with God will supply strength to keep us from temptation and protect us from Satan and evil. "And do not lead us into temptation, but deliver us from the evil one."

6. We pledge our faith and place our trust in the absolute supreme power and authority of our Lord and God. "For Yours is the kingdom and the power and the glory forever. Amen" (NKJV).

Help Us, Lord

In addition to Jesus' example and teaching on prayer, God also provides the Holy Spirit who helps us pray at times when we may feel unsure of how or what to pray. You can always ask the Holy Spirit to help you pray. Regarding prayer and the example that Jesus set, Mott wrote in 1910:

> It need only be added that Christians learn to pray not only from the teaching of Christ but possibly even more from His contagious example. The more fully His life of unbroken communion, as well as going apart for

special intercession, and His agonizing in the Garden on behalf of the world are studied, the more deeply will the Church enter into the secret of overcoming the world. Our duty to our generation involves a sense of spiritual responsibility that will open a Gethsemane wherever there is a Christian.

There are three very powerful descriptions of prayer captured in this statement. Prayer for all things at all times—unbroken communion—is a picture of prayer as a relationship-building tool with God. Then, there's special intercession, or calling on God to intervene and make a way wherever and whenever a way does not seem to exist. And finally, we are encouraged to join Jesus in His agony for a world that is lost to sin. Going to Gethsemane means placing yourself before God to accept the plan He has for your life to bring about His kingdom and reach lost souls.

> **"He that loseth his time for communion with God** shall find it again in added blessing, and power, and fruitfulness."[3]   **JRM**

Becoming disciplined in prayer requires a commitment to practice it every day. Mott encouraged us to jealously guard the time we set for prayer, and it only makes sense. Shouldn't our fellowship with our Creator always come first?

Let Us Commit to Prayer

Scripture teaches that, with God, all things are possible. So think for a moment: has God called you to a work that seems impossible, out of reach, or out of phase with reality? If yes, join the ranks of Abraham, Moses, David, Nehemiah, Mary, Peter, Paul and, of course, John R. Mott. In 1886, five days after God confirmed Mott's calling to be an evangelist, Mott admitted he was "an empty and broken vessel for the Master's use made weak."

In the face of God's divine calling, it is natural to feel weak and empty, both full of passion and excitement and unsure of your abilities or sure that you lack the ability. But it's not God's style to call the talented, competent, and self-assured. He calls those whose hearts are committed to seeking His will, though through human eyes we may seem unqualified. In 1 Corinthians 1:27, Paul says, "God has chosen the weak things of the world to shame things which are strong" (NASB). So, like Mott, accept the call and start seeking God's provision. And when we pray, let's be:

- Definite. Speak clearly defined prayers; do not be vague or general. Go to the Lord with specifics.
- Fervent. Earnestly express your feelings and hold nothing back. Pour out your heart to the Lord, and share your fears, pains, triumphs, and joy! Go to Gethsemane.
- Importunate. Pray continually. Develop an unbroken communion with God, punctuated by periods of focused intercession.

For it is in these things that the truest joy of all is found: intimate relationship with God and the chance to fulfill the plans He has for us. Remember: it is not He who waits to hear your call. It is He who is waiting for you to respond to His.

LESSON 6
IN REFLECTION

For Yourself

1. The Lord instructs us to pray continually. What would this look like in your daily life?
2. Does the phrase "too busy not to pray" fit your life?
3. How does prayer help you know God better?
4. Why did Jesus teach us to pray in solitude?

For Group Discussion and Leadership

1. In light of the author's thoughts, what role should prayer have in your organization?
2. Why do you think organizations ignore the role of prayer in their God-inspired work?
3. List the differences you would expect to see between an organization that has an active prayer life and one that doesn't.

7

Do "Multiplying" Work

by Doug Kohl

Imagine the scene: you're a fisherman, and you're preparing your net for the next big catch as the sun starts to rise. You quietly hope for an exceptional day, one in which the net will be full to overflowing, meaning not only food for you, but also provision for your family.

The day ahead is full of promise. And then, you hear the voice.

It is at once firm but inviting, both full of passion and full of peace. And it simply says, "Come, follow me."

The Scriptures tell us that when Jesus spoke those words, Simon and his brother Andrew put down their nets and did as He invited. They immediately left behind their livelihood, their families, and their individual hopes and dreams, just so they could volunteer.

Take a look around you. Who is there, just waiting to be asked?

It's so easy for us to take volunteers for granted, to think of them as expendable or replaceable, with not as much to offer as our trained, paid staff. But volunteers tend to have big dreams. They're often the ones who stand in the gaps, and do things for entirely different reasons than those on the payroll. I know this because that's how I, too, first became a part of the YMCA. As a teenager, I was asked to be part of a program committee so I agreed because I wanted to help. I know volunteers don't do things because they want recognition; they do things because they really want to help.

Multiplying Work

At our YMCA, there are about 550 employees, and more than two thousand volunteers. Around here, though, we consider them unpaid staff, and make sure to give them the training, encouragement, and direction they need to produce the desired outcomes.

Really, it's part of the legacy of the YMCA, and it's what John R. Mott called "multiplying work." Here's the concept: if you're going to reach thousands of children and families with the YMCA's Christian, faith-based values, you can do it much more effectively by involving volunteers than you can possibly do by yourself. What Mott referred to as multiplying work is really the empowerment of volunteers. In a strictly business sense, volunteers are the real stakeholders of any not-for-profit organization.

> **"Group thinking, planning, and acting constitute the** most highly multiplying method. Christ sent workers out two by two and in groups. We cannot know the full mind of our Lord or achieve the finest and largest results if we play a lone hand."[1] **JRM**

But on a grander scale, volunteers have been known to breathe life into those same organizations and turn mission statements into reality.

I've seen it with my own eyes. We just had a ribbon-cutting for a YMCA branch in northeastern Ohio, whose very existence goes back seven years to a time when three families sat around a dinner table at camp, asking why there wasn't a Y in their community.

The truth is we're surrounded by people with expertise in a great many things. But we, as leaders, need to develop Mott's concept of multiplying work. Rather than training our staff to teach, we should train volunteers to lead, involving them deeply in the work of the organization. And it all starts with a simple request: "Come, follow me."

Mott and Student Mobilization

Mott was known for his passion for evangelism. But just as important was his belief about the way the Great Commission—or taking the gospel of Christ into the world—was to be accomplished. He believed it would happen when young people were equipped to lead. His work with the YMCA student movement on college campuses was felt in all corners of America, as well as across the globe.

Over and over, Mott created forums and organizations that brought people together to work across religious, racial, and national boundaries. His life was rooted in the recognition that "in Christ there is no East or West." In his book *Five Decades and a Forward View*, Mott quoted Benjamin Disraeli saying, "It is a holy sight to see a nation saved by its youth." Because of that view, Mott's life was characterized by a commitment to develop younger leaders who would take Christ to every corner of the earth. Students were the hope for the world, and the universities and colleges were the fields where the finest could be challenged to serve Christ.

Steps in the Right Direction

The Bible talks about this equipping work. Jesus mentored, discipled, and encouraged people into positions of leadership. Jesus' goal was that the disciples would do even greater things then He, and Mott's model was that of Jesus Christ. As it says in John 14:12,

"I tell you the truth, whoever believes in me will do the same things that I do. Those who believe will do even greater things than these, because I am going to the Father" (NCV).

So how exactly does it work on a practical level?

First, it's important to recognize that people like to be asked. I don't believe there's an organization, church, or agency that doesn't have room for growth somewhere, so start looking around you. This helps you begin to establish a culture that both values and promotes multiplying work. Every bit of work within the organization should be connected to the concept that multiplying work is how the mission gets shared. Each published piece should reflect a commitment to the involvement of volunteers. Build multiplying work into job descriptions, performance appraisal instruments, and into the language of the organization.

In addition, get over the idea that if you simply do something yourself, it will be done more quickly. That doesn't allow others to become co-owners of your mission. Instead, offer responsibility, and when those tasks are completed, give full credit where credit is due.

Second, intentionally plan out what you hope to accomplish. All significant planning and vision documents should refer to the importance of involving volunteers in the work and ministry of the organization. This helps everyone get on board with the belief that volunteers are important.

Start with the mission statement, vision statement, and committee or task group commissions. Include volunteers—especially youth and young adults—in the process and on all committees. I already mentioned that we treat our volunteers as unpaid staff, and that's true; we want them to be in the middle of the action, rather than peripheral to it.

Third, set goals. Make them measurable, and make sure everyone knows what they are. By all means, put them in writing.

Fourth, write an action plan that describes where you have been in the past, where you are now, and where you hope to be in the future.

Fifth, recruit. But don't just ask people to volunteer. Ask people instead how they would like to make a difference. Again, people don't volunteer for recognition. They volunteer because they want to see the results of their contributions, so make sure they do. Make sure they know how very vital they are.

In his book *The Volunteer Revolution*, Bill Hybels puts it this way:

> The desire to be a world changer is planted into the heart of every human being and that desire comes directly from the heart of God. We can suffocate that desire in selfishness, silence it with the chatter of competing demands, or bypass it on the track to personal achievement. But it's still there. Whenever we wonder if the daily eight-to-five grind or our round-the-clock parenting tasks are all there is to life, that divine desire nudges us. Whenever we feel restless and unsatisfied, the desire whispers in our soul. Whenever we wonder what a life of real purpose would feel like, the desire calls us to something more.

Sixth, invest in your staff—paid and unpaid—by offering training and support. Getting the right person for any job is very important, but making the commitment to train and support the multiplying work is just as critical to success. Some will question how much time should be taken in this area, and may even ask if it's worth it if a volunteer is going to move on to another project or organization. But give this some thought. The only thing worse than training a volunteer and having them leave is not training them at all and having them stay.

Seventh, supervise volunteers as you would any staff person. Create job descriptions, meet regularly to assess progress, recognize and thank those who labor, and evaluate the results of the program or ministry. Track and chart the work and hours of the volunteers you involve. This is helpful for evaluation and planning as you move forward.

One more thing: if it's not working out, let them go. People think you can't fire a volunteer, but it may be the best thing for everyone involved.

In short, your volunteer program will be what you make it. There are great people in every community with exceptional talents who are willing to give their time as volunteers. They're looking for programs that make a difference, are well-organized, and will value their contributions. These people thrive on the energy generated by volunteering, and in turn, your organization will thrive on their energy, too. Together we can do far more for others than we can alone—and we can have a much better time doing it, as well.

The problem is that we often find a faithful core of people doing almost everything in an organization, while the vast majority observe or simply participate. What happens next is that those few can burn out, some even leaving in disaffection, feeling unneeded and left out. Because of that, we must be consistently vigilant to involve new members in our work. Our job as those involved in multiplying work is to give volunteers fulfilling jobs that they enjoy, making them an integral part of the programs they're working on.

Everyone at the Table

Please understand: volunteering is a necessary act of affirmation for any community. From barn raisings to church meetings to YMCA programs, these activities are integral to the human experience and essential to its societies.

One of the great concepts that the Christian faith has given to the world is that all people have worth and that their existence is important. Volunteers bring different perspectives to the issues they work on. Accomplishing a task can be debated from different points of view, and each and every person can contribute to the ultimate goal, whether that goal is to bring people to know Christ, to feed the hungry, to house the homeless, or to offer programs for children and families. Yet even in Christian-based organizations, it's easy to fall into that staff managerial model, in which staff are the ones making all the decisions.

The fact is that too often we don't take Mott's passion for including volunteers seriously. We don't trust them with the most important work of all: taking the mission of the organization out into the community and making it come alive for so many more people than one staff person could do alone. Too often, staff members think that they know best. And that's the kind of paternalism that absolutely intimidates and suppresses evangelism and stifles buy-in from the volunteers.

Instead, look at it this way: when you build a church, it's never really about the building. It's about the people. And organizations like the YMCA are the same way. In the YMCA, members are 99 percent of the constituency. It's not the staff's organization, but it's all of ours collectively; and as a result, volunteers should be in the thick of things. On a practical level, that may mean holding important meetings at times that are convenient for volunteers to attend, and not just staff. It may mean giving everybody the same kind of name tag, so volunteers feel as important as paid staff. And it certainly means listening to their input, and being open to new ideas and new directions that we might not have thought of ourselves.

As volunteers become multiplying instruments, they experience a level of fulfillment they hope will never end, so they win, too. And the surrounding community wins as it is served by a unified, multi-gifted force for good. The YMCA's Christian heritage bears much resemblance to the church roots that birthed it. People like Mott had a vision grounded in a common set of values, and he made sure that those values were shared with the world through the work and ministry of the organization.

Our mandate, then, is equally clear. We are to be people of God—a fellowship of believers—intentionally involving ourselves in ongoing acts of caring, honesty, respect, and responsibility, in God's name, in our homes, in our congregations, in our organizations, and in the world.

And we most certainly can't do that on our own.

LESSON 7
IN REFLECTION

For Yourself

1. Outside your job, how do you do multiplying work for God?
2. Who could you ask to join you in the multiplying work to be done?
3. What God-given gifts do you have to offer to others?
4. What do you consider to be the common values grounded in Christian faith that we are called forth to multiply?

For Group Discussion and Leadership

1. How important are volunteers to the organization you work for?
2. Is it more important to recruit a volunteer to do the job that needs to be done or to create a job that is most appropriate for the person who wants to volunteer? Why?
3. Does your organization see volunteers as essential to the work and ministry to be accomplished in the world or as a waste of time and a risk?
4. Is your organization volunteer-friendly? Do you make room for volunteers with different gifts? How about minorities or those with special needs?
5. Do volunteers care more about the what, when, and where details, or do they care about the mission of the organization? Where and how do you want your volunteers to express their care?

8

Use the "Heroic Appeal"

*A heroic appeal often gets a heroic response.
It is good to have difficulties because it
calls out the most in you, it drives you to get the
cooperation of others, it drives you to God.*

JRM

by Tim Joyce

Camp to me was more than just "camp."

It was a place I always knew I would have the same bed, and I would wake up surrounded by others who valued and accepted me. It wasn't so much like that at home.

But it was also the place something else happened: it was the place I met a group of amazing men, four directors we irreverently called "the God Squad." They were father figures to me, men who exemplified the teachings of the Scriptures, and lived lives of integrity and responsibility. They were men who became my heroes.

Funny thing is, I wasn't at camp to be a camper. We never could afford it when I was growing up, and since my parents were estranged, my sister was fifteen years older, and my mom couldn't handle me on her own, I missed some family dynamics that others probably took for granted.

So it wasn't until I graduated high school, when all my friends went off for beach retreats, that I decided to go to work at the YMCA's Camp Sea Gull. That meant cabins full of seven-year-olds, and it was the first time in my life I was responsible for someone other than myself. It was the greatest time of maturation in my life. Thankfully, I had those heroes on hand to show me how it should be done. And one of the ways they did that was to live lives that pointed me to the ultimate hero, Jesus Christ.

The Source of Strength

Think of the word hero and, no doubt, you'll conjure up mighty warriors straining against all odds to win the cause, or the down-and-out underdog battling to defeat the Goliath challenger. You might even think of the average John Doe who goes beyond his normal and usual abilities to respond in a way that brings healing or peace to someone else.

All of these heroes have something in common: they're heroes because they've risen to the occasion at hand and have overcome whatever difficulties that faced them in order to do so.

The more I read about John R. Mott, the more of a hero he becomes to me, too. He accomplished a great many things in his life, overcoming any situation to move toward his ultimate goal: reaching the world for Christ. And because of that, I believe he truly understood the idea of the "heroic appeal" and the "heroic response." And he, too, understood the source from which true heroism comes: relationship with God.

I know all too well how rich a source that is. You see, my second child, my son Russell, was born with birth defects. When you don't have a perfect Gerber baby, you can really hit the bottom. And that's exactly what I did. The Lord and I had it out that day in the hospital chapel.

Over the years, however, I saw that He was giving me a heroic appeal. And He gave me the chance to have a heroic response. Now hear me closely: I don't really consider myself a hero. But now that Russell is an extremely healthy teen, I can look back at all of those years He gave me strength to stand, to continue to ask for my son's healing, and to believe it would come to pass.

Every night, I would go to bed asking God to make Russell whole. I always wanted to wake up the next day and see that everything was in place. And one day, when Russell was fourteen, it all of a sudden hit me that he was indeed whole. God had healed holes in my son's heart. He had turned him into an athlete who walked just fine, even though he had been diagnosed with scoliosis. And He gave him a compassion for others that you wouldn't believe, just because of everything he'd been through. Can I take credit for that because I answered God's heroic appeal? Not really. But I can say that, through the goodness of God, our lives will never be the same.

> **"Here lies also one of the essential secrets of winning** to the cause the oncoming generation. They need a challenge vast enough to appeal to the imagination, and exacting and heroic enough to call out their adventurous spirit and their latent energies."[1]   **JRM**

I recently took one of those tests on spiritual gifts, and one of my highest category scores was for faith. Until recently, I never really considered faith a strong spiritual gift, but I know now that other people would disagree. It's like they say, the more you go through, the stronger you get. He only gives us what we can handle. At the time, it may feel like there's no way you can handle a situation, but before you know it, you're looking back from the other side and you can clearly see God's hand at work.

The Appeal Is Made

In my case, the heroic appeal came directly from God. But every culture, religion, society, and nation has heroes that have mounted heroic appeals of their own. Webster's dictionary defines heroic as "marked with great courage and daring," "grand," and "noble." In reading this definition, it's easy to think of, for example, David battling Goliath, George Washington crossing the Delaware, Abraham Lincoln struggling to maintain the Union,

John Glenn blasting off into space, or the soldiers of D-Day and Iwo Jima fighting to suppress evil tyrannies. It could also be the quiet resolve of the Pilgrims coming to a new land to start a new life, Jesus Christ in the upper room with His disciples, Mother Teresa ministering in the streets of Calcutta, or Billy Graham on his endless circuit proclaiming the Word of God. Unfortunately, history has shown us leaders with misguided heroic appeals, as well; consider Ahab and Jezebel, Hitler, or Stalin. Each one of them, whether their appeal was good or bad, spoke volumes just through the example of their lives, not to mention the causes that they represented.

> **"The heroic appeal makes possible the heroic response.** The strongest men can be inspired to accomplishment by putting before them something that is really baffling and truly significant."[2]   **JRM**

But whatever your image of the heroic appeal, the impact is almost always the same. When we choose to give the heroic response, we're moved deep within our souls, our heartbeat quickens, and our palms may even sweat as we swing into action. We become inspired, passionate, and willing to rally for a cause bigger than ourselves, whether it's overcoming a perceived obstacle, oppression, or weakness; we stand up to a bully or evil persuasion; we "boldly go where no man has gone before." And the final result is the overcoming of insurmountable odds to achieve something that was originally seen as being impossible to do. Again, think of Mott and his passion for every lost soul.

Room for God to Work

Ever hear of Franklin Graham? He's the son of Billy Graham, and he likes to talk about "God room." I like to talk about it, too, because it's a great example of a heroic response and appeal—and one that I think even Mott could relate to.

The idea is that no matter what we do, we should allow for God room, or plan for things to happen that only God can bring about. In other words, we give God room to work. At the YMCA, it's become one of our customs to ask where the God room is. And we ask the question: if God removed His hand, what are we doing right now that could no longer be done? We hope, a lot! This is the place where, as an organization, godly vision can step in and work through people's hearts. Of course, it means really slowing down, and taking the time to listen and pray. It also means we end up doing some risky stuff, such as sending our buses into some tough areas in order to serve youth and families, taking part in gang interventions, and shooting for the moon in our annual fundraising efforts.

> **"Love breaking out in enthusiasm and sacrifice for** great unselfish causes never fails to attract, to convince, and to set aflame. It is the impossible situation and the program this world calls impossible which makes possible the fresh and larger conceptions and manifestations of the Creative God."[3]   **JRM**

But it sure makes things exciting. And isn't that what heroism is all about? Now, history has been filled with heroes who have risen up to speak, act, or encourage others in an appeal to rally them for a cause. But as life would teach us, most of the humans walking the earth don't think they have much in common with heroes who accomplish great feats. As such, I love the words of Helen Keller when she said,

> The world is not moved along by the mighty shoves of its heroes but more so by the collective tiny nudges of its ordinary man.

That ordinary man is me. In my eyes, I'm pretty insignificant. But in the eyes of those in need who are hungry, thirsty, naked, sick, or imprisoned, I'm a hero who moves the very foundations of the earth.

Go ahead, be honest. Don't you just wish that once, just once, you could spin a web and swing like Spiderman? Or fly like Superman? Or have the wisdom of Solomon? In truth, most of us are just everyday people; we're not the legends of lore listed above. But, as we learn to walk with God, as individuals and as an organization, we discover opportunities to rise to the occasion. And until that happens, we simply don't realize the power that we have.

The Step of Faith

Our family loves to watch movies. One of the greatest visuals that comes to mind when I think of heroism is in Harrison Ford's third Indiana Jones movie, *The Last Crusade*. In case you don't remember, I'll help set the scene. Indiana Jones is trying to get to the Holy Grail. To do so, he has to pass through an obstacle course constructed by those of Jesus' time to protect the chalice from any ordinary man. The Grail, as legend had it, would give immortality to anyone who drank from it. Indy has to get the Grail, and fast, because his father has been shot and lay dying. A drink from the Grail will heal him.

The last test to reach the Grail is to "take a step of faith." He stands looking across a chasm too wide to jump, with nothing to propel him and only his father's notes from years of study to get him through the test. So he takes a deep breath and steps over the ledge. And to his amazement, he's caught by a land bridge, invisible to the eye. Needless to say, the relief on his face goes without description.

But, isn't that how it is in our moments of great trial or dilemma? We take these final, gasping steps of faith only to be caught by what we cannot see, that being God's plan, provision, and mercy. Our senses don't pick up on God's provision because God is spirit, where we are full of instinct and sensory perception. How often have we been urged to "not be afraid" and "have the faith of a mustard seed," and yet we don't? Instead we thrash around trying to do it our way. And then, only when we have come to the final chapter and are unable to solve the issue on our own, we step out. But in order for us to take this step out of our comfort zone or this step to meet the crisis in our lives, we must allow the heroic appeal to move us.

The Appeal of Esther

Next time you or your organization faces a task that seems insurmountable, consider Esther. She was approached by Mordecai, her counselor, about an evil plot to kill all the Hebrews of the time. As queen, she might be able to get the king to change his mind. The fact that she was queen was one of God's mighty provisions; she was put in that position for the very moment at hand. Yet, even as queen, she was restricted from approaching the king without his permission.

What would have happened if she had said, "No, not me. Some other hero will have to step up to do the task. I'm not risking the chance of my head and neck becoming prematurely separated." I believe God would have acted through another if Esther had chosen not to respond to the heroic appeal of Mordecai, and in another way. But Esther is blessed among men and women for her heroic response at the moment of crisis. And what was that heroic response? She approached the king and laid out for him the conspiracy threatening his kingdom. Nothing mighty, strong, or massive in operation. She just gave an honest heroic appeal of her own.

Mordecai, too, brought forth the original heroic appeal that brought Esther to action. He couldn't come before the king himself. He couldn't even come inside the palace unless invited. Even Esther couldn't approach the king without being summoned. But she at least had a chance. Mordecai had to bring the truth and the appeal to Esther to move her heart to action to bring the appeal to the king.

When it was all said and done, Mordecai was honored by the king as a hero for past acts and loyalty. The man Haman, who plotted to kill Mordecai and the Hebrews, was hung from the very gallows built for Mordecai's execution. See, God has a way of blessing those who serve Him. You may not be the final voice that saves the cause, wins the battle, or solves the mystery, but you may still get to be the hero by giving an appeal that touches the heart and spurs another to action.

I believe that's the way it was in 1844, when George Williams saw a need and put forth a heroic appeal to those he knew to come help him combat the ravages of social decadence in London, England. In so doing, he created this organization called the Young Men's Christian Association. His basis was found in the writings of a certain Jewish carpenter who said, "that they may be one as we are one: I in them and you in me" (John 17:21 NIV). Since then, unimaginable good and ministry has come from this organization over the years. As the oldest social service organization in the world, it's hard not to stand in awe of the appeal and the continued power it has upon those who serve in it and are served by it.

Getting Out of the Goat Herd

Yet even with all of our success over the years, it's still possible for us to miss the boat. In our association, we constantly question each other and urge ourselves to remember what brought us here in the first place. We ask, "Why do you do what you do? You could go to any other business, work fewer hours, with less stress, and maybe even make more money. So why do you do it?" It must be the heroic appeal of service to our brothers and sisters. But the true appeal, the one that motivates so many of us, comes from that same Jewish carpenter in a parable He shared with the people of His time. Jesus was speaking of eternal life and living forever in the company of God, the great Creator of all things. He painted a picture of separating sheep and goats into two pens, a visible image the people of the day could understand. He continued, saying how those standing in the goat herd (not the place you want to be) became indignant about their location and inquired why. This carpenter's words echo through the ages with the power of a mighty sledgehammer. He told them they were in the goat herd because when He was hungry, they brought Him nothing to eat. When He was thirsty, they brought Him nothing to drink. When He was naked and cold, they did not clothe Him. When He was in prison and when He was sick, they did not come to Him. Their response was, "When did we see you like this? We would certainly have ministered to you."

But the appeal here was His answer, and it truly must be the reason we do what we do: "Inasmuch as you did it to one of the least of these My brethren, you did it to Me" (Matt. 25:40 NKJV).

Along the way, we don't always know how God will work, but we do have a choice in whether or not we answer His heroic appeals, whether they come directly from Him or through someone else. Our job is just to take a step of faith. God will work out the rest.

We must realize it is the tiny, everyday heroic appeals that move people and organizations to fulfill God's master plan. So, what is your appeal to others, and how do you respond to the appeals that come to you? Are you too busy to listen? Too busy to engage? Do you say, "Here's a check; I'll support your cause," when what they need is your time and your expertise?

Granted, we can't respond to every need that comes along, but the Lord will help us discern what we should do. But it's important to remember that it's the small, everyday tasks done in heroic faith that win the day. And no one knows the impact those tasks can have on others.

Ah, the heroic appeal in everyday life. It's not a Hollywood epic movie, not a story of legend or lore, but just a simple life of courage, faith, and perseverance. It's simply the aggregate of the "tiny nudges" of the common everyday person. That same Jewish carpenter said, "Let your light so shine before men that they may see your good works and glorify your Father in heaven" (Matt. 5:16 NKJV). So, what heroic appeal has been brought to you that you're wrestling with answering? What about your life or organization's ministry is a heroic appeal to someone else? And most of all, what are you doing about it?

LESSON 8
IN REFLECTION
For Yourself

1. Describe a time you overcame the odds to do something very difficult. Did you turn to God? Why?
2. What about your life is a heroic appeal to someone else? What are you doing about it?
3. What heroic appeal has been placed on your heart by God that you are wrestling with?

For Group Discussion and Leadership

1. Think of a change your organization needs to make. How can a heroic appeal play a role?
2. Describe a difficult time for your organization's history. How did this difficult time:
   • call out the most in your leadership, staff, and volunteers?
   • drive you to seek the cooperation of others?
   • drive you to God?
3. Based on your answers to the question above, what implications does this have for the next difficulty your organization experiences?

9

Strategy Is Important

*There are strategic points which if captured, make easy
all that lies behind them. There are strategic classes and
strategic races, strategic times, strategic methods,
strategic places. We must know what they are.*

JRM

by Tom Massey

Most people know the story of the guy walking along the beach after a storm who sees the young man throwing starfish back into the ocean. The guy says, "Why are you throwing one starfish at a time back into the ocean—there are too many starfish on the shore for you to make a difference." The young man poetically replies, "I am making a difference for this one" as he flings another into the sea.

Many people identify with the young man. They work hard everyday to make a difference in the lives of people. The world would be a very sad place without such people.

But I identify with the other guy. I don't know why, but I am wired to say, "Wait a minute, if keeping starfish alive is important, let's get serious about this." I think strategy is important, even when doing good . . . maybe especially when using limited resources to do good. Here's how it would unfold:

I would have snapped a picture of the starfish with my cell phone. I would have sent the picture and a broadcast voice/text message to my friends. I would tell them to meet me at the beach. Next a call to the aquatics director at the Y asking her to bring all the lost and found towels, sunscreen, and her rescue tube (in case some volunteers get in a little too deep).

By then I would be back to my car where I would have fired up my satellite laptop. I would Google the nearest college marine biology department, go into their chat room or blog, upload my photo, and outline the plight of these starfish. I would tell them to come help us fix this situation, or at least email me the right way to do it. Maybe tossing starfish isn't so good for them—I don't know.

Then back to the beach to gather the starfish into piles while waiting on the troops. Once a few arrived, we would have taken a minute to assess the situation, pool our knowledge, set a plan, make assignments, and then get to work putting the starfish back in the sea. This strategic session would have taken under ten minutes.

After we finished, there would be photos of the team on the clear beach and talk of meeting again after the next storm. I am sure one of the computer geeks would have volunteered to establish a listserv. Knowing my friend who owns the sporting goods store, T-shirts with a starfish logo would be on the way that week. I would have ended the day by contacting that marine biology department and asking what causes the starfish to wash ashore. Is this just a natural occurrence? Is an artificial reef needed on that particular stretch of beach? What foundations fund this sort of thing?

Individual, hard work is needed, important, and makes a difference in the lives of many. Hard work as part of a group—strategically planned, organized, and deployed—can change the world.

The Nuts and Bolts

John R. Mott makes it sound so simple. I love his faith in the "strategic points" that make everything else easy. But let's back up and lay some groundwork before we get there.

First, the obligatory definition: strategy can be defined many ways, and is often used as a synonym for "plan." The problem with that is we use the word "plan" in a lot of ways that aren't very strategic. We plan, for example, to go on a vacation somewhere, sometime. Our plan is to make as much money as possible. We plan to seize every opportunity. The company has a plan to react to every contingency.

Let's stretch that definition a little by adding the word "priority." A strategy can be thought of as a priority plan. We can do lots of things, but what are the most important things to do, to move us toward our vision? If our options are A and B, which is the better choice? When we make this type of decision based on our vision, it becomes strategic thinking.

I'll be honest. Given a choice between attending a strategic planning session and having a root canal, I'll most likely be on my way to the dentist. I never understood how twenty well-meaning people in the same room could spend two-thirds of their time writing a mission statement that nobody really understood, and end up with only a completely unexciting, dispassionate experience.

Have any idea what I'm talking about?

Sure you do. We've all been there, wanting to do "good," wanting to make a difference, but still not exactly sure how. It's time, then, for me to let you in on a little secret: God already has it all figured out. All we have to do is catch His vision and set a strategy, and we really can change the world.

God and Strategy

Some may be offended by the idea that God has a strategy, but I think most would agree that God does have a priority plan. The Bible says we may not always understand it, like it, or even be aware of it—but we have faith that God's ways are above our ways.

We know God's priority plan was to have a wonderful relationship with people—one based on free choice. But we certainly messed that up from the start. Thank goodness it was not an absolute plan and God was willing to give us another path to achieve that same vision. Grace covers bad strategy.

Now, as a consultant, I help churches and Christian organizations like the YMCA plan. Inevitably, someone will say something like, "We don't need to plan so much that we can't respond to God's Spirit."

Personally, I find several things challenging about that statement. First, I plan on listening and responding to God's Spirit during the planning process. I'm reasonably sure God can speak to us in a planning room with the same clarity and conviction as when we're engaged in the work.

> **"The world situation as it exists today summons us as** Christian forces to much more comprehensive plans. How inadequate our plans are! How unworthy they are of such a great Savior and of His illimitable resources!"[1]   **JRM**

Second, I'm not sure I can always distinguish between hearing God's Spirit and my own personal biases, agendas, and preferences. But with a group of wise people all seeking the right path, I have much more confidence in determining the will of God.

And finally, if we are sure God's Spirit is moving us in a direction different from our strategic plan, of course, I am going to make a change. There are times when the best thing to do is make a bonfire with all the planning documents to light the way down another path.

Let's talk a little bit more about prayer here, since it should be part of that entire process. I don't know how you can do much of anything without it, either personally or corporately. If you truly want God's vision and strategy for your organization, prayer must be a priority. I'm certain Mott, man of God that he was, would agree.

If we seek first the Kingdom, as it tells us in the Scriptures, everything else will fall into place.

Now, before we move on, I'd also like to challenge the idea that just because an organization is a "ministry," it doesn't have to be held to the same set of organizational standards as a secular agency. Are we not compelled to do things with excellence so that He can be glorified? Are we not motivated to do things that make those in the world sit up and take notice?

Finding Purpose and More

Through the years, I've come across four points of strategic planning that can help organizations and people get where they want to go. Each one requires careful reflection, study, decisions, and action, but the results can be better than you can imagine. I developed this four-point planning process for organizations, but I've modified it here to serve as a resource for your personal walk with God. So let's dive in.

First, there's purpose. A purpose may last a lifetime, or at least a significant portion of one. Purpose can be modified along the way. Next, there are principles. These are based on long-held beliefs that rarely change. Third, there are priorities, which can last for years, but do change due to life situations, accomplishments, and new challenges. And finally, there's performance, which focuses on the day-to-day.

> **"A man may be a strategist without being a leader,** but no leader can exert the maximum influence—that is, render the maximum service—who is not also a good strategist."[2]   **JRM**

Now, let's look at each point a little more in-depth. We'll start with purpose. Most organizations (and some people) have mission statements, but a statement of purpose is different. It should be clear, concise, compelling—but not necessarily comprehensive. Some of the most powerful ones I've seen are just two words long. They include, for example, "love God," "serve others," "lead wisely," and "share grace." Each represents a central cause, why you do the things you do. It is your ultimate rudder and compass, not to mention your reason for being.

Personally, my purpose statement is "to have a closer relationship with God." I couldn't make it two words and still convey all I wanted. Since I can always get closer no matter where I am in my relationship with God, it has continually challenged me for most of my adult life. It calls me to action.

However, I can't make everything I do in my life fit under that purpose statement. I guess I should, but not everything I do at work is necessarily helping my relationship with God. I do go to a movie sometimes. I may even obsess over sports from time to time. I refuse to be one of those people who rationalizes or plays games to make everything fit. Taking a nap could be listed as gaining the energy I need to serve God better. But more than likely, it's because I stayed up too late on Saturday watching college football and a rainy Sunday afternoon seems to make being lazy okay.

Principles

Now, let's consider those principles. They're different than values. Values are important to have and to demonstrate. Often values are good, and to choose something else would be bad. Need an example? Be honest; don't lie. Principles, on the other hand, are ideals that you've chosen to use in making decisions, choices, and setting priorities. Your operating principles may be perfect for you or your organization, but someone else can have an equally fruitful life choosing an opposite principle.

For example, spending time on Bible study and serving those in need are both important to my purpose of having a closer relationship with God, and I intend to apply both principles for the rest of my life. But I don't have unlimited time, energy, resources, passion, or spiritual giftedness. So, if I have spare time beyond my regular Bible study and service commitments, I choose to spend that time serving those in need instead of more Bible study. Some of this principle is about where I am in my life. When I was younger, I found Bible study helped me more. I could learn things and apply them with my family, church, and work. But now, I find I feel closer to God through more service opportunities. I have even talked with my small Bible study group about taking on projects, helping the poor instead of just meeting, studying, and discussing.

When you sit down and write out a list of principles, remember to keep the list short. Do you think you can you really focus and apply more than six principles regularly and in most aspects of your life? Remember, don't try for comprehensiveness—just focus on areas that are important to you. Now, could these change? Absolutely. Could God redirect you? Of course.

The idea of operating principles, however, can be essential in how we use our resources as individuals and organizations. Should we pray about it? A lot. Should we seek the input of others? Many times. Are we open to direction from God? I'd hope so. But for now, we should look at the principles we've set and operate by those.

Priorities

I don't know about you, but I need a shorter list of priorities. I would love to do lots of things—but it turns out I can't. Plus, I wouldn't be as good at some things as I would others. Again, I have a finite amount of time, energy, passion, resources, and skills.

The same thing is true when it comes to running an organization. We can't be all things to all people, so we have to consider what's most important. Making a list of possible priorities, then, can be a good place to start. For a faith-based organization like the YMCA, the list might include providing programs for school-age children or giving the elderly a place to go. It might mean offering Bible studies or spiritual guidance, as well as offering the latest in physical fitness equipment.

Of course, everything on the list can be a good thing. And chances are, they're all connected to your purpose and principles. They may all, in one way or another, have value in God's Kingdom.

So how do we pick?

Put everything on the list into one of four categories: "priority," which should receive top consideration for time, effort, and resources; "reduced," which should receive less consideration in all those areas; "sequenced," which should receive future consideration; and "ongoing," which should receive the same consistent consideration. Help delineate by asking a few questions. How high is our passion level in this area? Do we have spiritual gifts or special ability in this area? How critical is the need in the next three years? Are there others who could do this better?

Put as many areas as you can in ongoing, so you can keep working on these things, but not at any increased level. Then, see what you can sequence for the future, put at least one area in the reduced category, and set your sights on the priorities.

Performance

Finally, let's develop a performance plan for those areas in the priority box. For each one, answer these questions:

- What is our specific vision for this area? Describe it as a complete success a few years from now.
- What are the key objectives in this area? Break the area down into smaller, more specific parts.
- How will we measure success in this area? What are some specific outcomes that will indicate the vision and key objectives are met?

- How does this priority area work with other priority or ongoing areas? Are there any synergies? Are there things we must stop doing or change to make this area a success?

Making It Real

Feel a little overwhelmed? Take a deep breath and relax. This is just a guideline. Remember to approach it all with prayer, and keep in mind the end results. And one more thing: Be sure it write it all down. (Habakkuk 2:2 urges us to "Write the vision; make it plain upon tablets, so he may run who reads it." That's great insight from an unknown author writing more than twenty-five hundred years ago.) Maybe you won't answer every single question, but at least get enough on paper to formulate a strategy. Sometimes notebooks or even full sheets of paper are intimidating, so consider index cards instead.

> **"To a clear sense of direction and of mission growing** out of unswerving loyalty to a common end, to wise guiding principles, to God-inspired objectives, and to our Divine Lord may be traced the marked success of co-operation, often in the face of the most baffling difficulties and opposition."[3] **JRM**

I can attest to the power of writing things down—even in spiritual matters. On a personal level, I've been journaling for a number of years, and I can't imagine my walk with God without it. Every year I start a new journal, and incorporate this four-point process for my life. My weekly and daily entries keep my strategies before me, and promote both accountability and authenticity.

If you're following these suggestions for your organization, though, make sure you and the others on your team hold each other accountable. Especially if you really mean business. Put priority planning to the test. God will help because strategy is important to Him.

For he has made known to us in all wisdom and insight the mystery of his will according to his purpose which he set forth in Christ as a plan for the fullness of time, to unite all things in him, things in heaven and things on earth (Eph. 1:9–10 NASB).

LESSON 9
IN REFLECTION

For Yourself

1. What is your personal "purpose" statement?
2. List six principles by which to live your life.
3. What priorities or goals have you set regarding your relationship with God? How will you commit to accomplishing them?

For Group Discussion and Leadership

1. Can you succinctly describe your organization's purpose? Would it inspire others to follow your organization's lead?
2. List the core principles that drive decisions in your organization. How many of these trace back to God's Word?
3. List three to five key priorities for your organization. How do they relate back to the foundation of your organization as you described it in Lesson 1?

10

We Need to Get into the Field

You cannot develop a Christian from an office chair. We need to be out meeting and dealing with personalities.

JRM

by Paul McEntire

Let me tell you about my mom.

She lives in North Carolina, and she walks two or three miles every day of her life. But until she came to visit me, she'd never set foot on a treadmill.

She was about seventy then, and while in town, she asked me if I would take her to one of the YMCA facilities. The whole thought of going into the unfamiliar territory of a fitness facility alone scared her—and frankly, her fear surprised me. People come in and out of our doors every day, and I'd never given it a second thought.

But the experience opened my eyes. Since I was there to see it firsthand—and to see it from her viewpoint—a couple of things became evident. We needed to rethink the way we had positioned some of our exercise machines so they were a little less intimidating, and we needed to make sure that we made things as easy as we could for those who were out of place. From that point on, for example, we began buying treadmills with easier-to-use controls. That way, they wouldn't put off someone who was used to another model at another facility, not to mention someone like my mother, who wasn't used to treadmills at all.

Guaranteed, had I been in my office that day rather than in the fitness room, nothing would ever have changed.

John R. Mott reminds us that we can't develop others while seated behind our desks, and I wholeheartedly agree. Getting out to where the people are is an essential part of meeting their needs. Otherwise, how can we really know what their needs are? The work we do in the YMCA is primarily people work, and the opportunities to be with those people are endless. There are schools, ball fields, wellness centers, gymnasiums, churches, community events, meetings, workplaces—the list goes on and on. But how do we reach people strategically, in a way that really meets them wherever they are?

The Biblical Basis

Though Mott's great evangelistic efforts proved that he valued getting out to the people, he wasn't the one who came up with the idea. We can find at least a couple of references in the Bible about reaching outside ourselves and our communities to touch others for Christ. Certainly the best known is Matthew 28:19–20, which commands, "Go therefore and make disciples of all the nations, baptizing them in the name of the Father and the Son and the Holy Spirit, teaching them to observe all I have commanded you; And lo, I am with you always, even to the end of the age" (NASB). It's a great passage, but the verb "go" is more accurately translated "as you are going." While the difference seems subtle, the change puts the primary focus on disciple making and the secondary focus on going. This keeps the responsibility more focused on all Christians, not just those able to go off to distant lands.

And then there's Acts 1:8, which says, "But you will receive power when the Holy Spirit has come upon you; and you shall be My witnesses in Jerusalem, and in all Judea and Samaria, and even to the remotest part of the earth" (NASB). This passage emphasizes that outreach begins first for Christians in their own backyards, and progresses to more distant places.

So how does this apply to the mission and action of people in faith-based organizations like the YMCA? The assumption is that Christian people will be on the go, and that as we are going, we will be doing God's work. The challenge before us, then, is to make sure we are regularly on the go and not stuck in our offices.

Beyond the Walls

On a practical level, there are many ways an organization can reach beyond its own walls. We have a program, for example, called Mission in Motion. Many churches in our area have extra space that isn't fully utilized during the week. As such, we've partnered with them to offer group classes and senior events for people in their communities. Under the plan, everybody benefits. The churches win because they're being good stewards of their empty facilities. The participants win because they're improving their health. And on our end, we have the opportunity to touch people—people like my own mother—who would go to the familiar setting of a church building, but who would be completely intimidated by the idea of the gym.

In addition, we offer Lunch and Learn classes, through which we partner with area businesses that have wellness programs. We also operate wellness centers in four different offices nearby, as well as after-school child care programs, mentoring programs, and other events.

Again, spending time with the people you want to reach can give you a much better idea of how to reach them more effectively. But it's not always as simple as just walking out your door; first, you have to determine who it is you want to serve.

Within a typical organization, I would suggest thinking about three primary groups of people whom we ought to serve. The "Golden Rule" can easily become a trite expression rather than the reality of how we live life, but it's still the standard by which we ought to evaluate our behavior. When considering how best to serve others, then, we have to ask ourselves: what would I want these people to do for me, if our roles were reversed?

> **"We need to come into heart-to-heart contact with the** real need of individual men (and at times in their humblest walks of life) and try to meet their need. We have so much platform and executive work that there is a real danger that we may lose the power of sympathy and tenderness which comes from seeking to bring the life of Christ into the lives of others by personal work."[1]   **JRM**

The first group is staff. Jesus set an incredible example for us in His multifaceted ministry to the disciples. By nurturing, training, and caring for the disciples, Jesus made sure they stayed equipped in every way to serve others. Any employee can do that for his or her fellow workers, but this is especially true for those in leadership positions who lead by being first a servant.

The second group is the members and participants of your group, in our case, YMCA members. These people have already chosen to become an active part of the YMCA community. By regularly reminding ourselves to view these people not as customers but as members of the YMCA community, we can keep our focus on serving these individuals through their involvement. Again, the Scriptures give us a glimpse of a group of people larger than the twelve disciples that were part of Jesus' life, and we get snippets of the ways Jesus interacted with and ministered to these people in an ongoing way. We have a similar opportunity with those who are active in our YMCAs.

The third group is those people who cross our path every day. Each day our lives are filled with divine opportunities. By being aware of and sensitive to God's leading, we can seize these moments in time whenever and wherever they come to us. Have you ever wondered why Jesus didn't heal everyone who was sick when He was alive? Why didn't He have a meal with each family, teach each person, or, in some way, express love to everyone? The quick answer is that, like us, Jesus lived His earthly life within the constraints of time and space. But the Scriptures give us a number of examples of those whose paths crossed Jesus' path, and then they became the beneficiaries of His ministry. Likewise, we have opportunities to impact the people who come in and out of our lives each day.

In Service to Others

Once we've figured out our audience, we must determine how to serve it in a way that meets the need of the moment. The apostle Paul, in Ephesians 1:18, prayed that the eyes of our hearts would be "enlightened." If we make this prayer a regular part of our own days, we will indeed become more aware of the needs around us, as well as creative ways of meeting them. For most of us, the key is simply to listen, which starts first with paying attention to what is going on around us. In our busyness, it's so easy to become self-focused. And being significantly self-focused can be as harmful to serving others as being selfish. Even if our hearts are soft and we're prompted to help someone in need, that heart can't help us at all if we're oblivious to the need all around us. People consistently ask for help in their own ways. We need to hone our listening skills so we hear and respond.

But in listening and responding, we need to pay attention to maintaining a humble spirit, as well. Philippians 2:3–4 guides us well with this: "Do nothing from selfishness or empty conceit, but with humility of mind regard one another as more important than yourselves; do not merely look out for your own personal interests, but also for the interests of other" (NASB).

In my own life, I've developed a spiritual discipline that helps me in my efforts toward humility. I call it "secret service." Much like prayer, Bible study, fasting, and other acts function as spiritual disciplines that God uses to conform us into the person He wants us to be, so committing acts of service without being known can assist in conforming us to God's image.

Practically speaking, this means looking for opportunities to do simple things for others without anyone knowing that you've done them. It may sound simple, but I suspect that if you give it a serious attempt you will find it more complex than you thought. Why? Because the human part of each of us is sinful and selfish. When we do find a good deed to do for someone, we want others to notice and applaud. If you doubt that you are like this, I encourage you to try it.

> **"By the test of generations and centuries it has not** been those who exercised lordship, dictatorship, or the dominance of human force over men, who won the deepest allegiance of the people of their day, and are today remembered with deepest gratitude; but rather those who absolutely forgot or lost themselves in great unselfish causes, or in lives abounding in countless little selfless deeds, and whose controlling ambition was to render the maximum helpfulness, especially to those in deepest need."[2]
>
> **JRM**

Here's a real example from my own life—albeit an embarrassing one—so you'll see what I mean. I was at a birthday gathering of seven families, including our youth minister and his family. It was a restaurant where you pay your money, take your seat, and go through a buffet line. I wanted to pay for the youth minister and his family, because I knew the cost for them was significant in relation to their budget. The youth minister walked past the cashier to the area set aside for the party where people were already beginning to eat. I told the cashier there were three of them and I would pay. The cashier rang it up, and I paid. The youth minister must have thought the host family had paid for everyone because he never made an attempt to pay. The party ended and we all departed. I had done what I thought was a quite generous thing, and no one, I mean no one, knew what I did. Biblically, I should have been experiencing joy from my act of giving. Sinfully, I was upset that my good deed had elicited not even the smallest acknowledgment.

Regrettably, I always find that at some level I feel cheated when I provide secret service and it really does remain a secret. This reminds me that even my good deeds can have selfish motives. The act of looking for opportunities for secret service also helps me be aware of more ways I can serve anonymously as well as publicly.

On a Practical Level

Part of the benefit of being with others is that we can help meet needs as they arise. But that's not all there is to it. Reaching others can also mean developing and following a plan that helps create opportunity. Jesus clearly did this as He organized His disciples, planned and organized ministry trips, trained and prepared His disciples, sent them out on mission, and followed up with evaluation and debriefing, as it tells us in Luke 10:1–24 when He sent out the seventy-two. The possibilities in this area are unlimited.

As an individual—or an organization—then, start by taking some quiet, reflective time to prepare your heart. Involve others, and together, you can seek God's guidance on what types of ministry to move into.

YMCAs are filled with examples. I have seen several YMCAs start angel tree programs to provide toys to children and families in need. At two locations I'm familiar with, the programs grew from a dozen or so families to more than one hundred in just a couple of years. A group of volunteers and staff at another YMCA started a day care program for handicapped young adults who no longer qualify for services by their school district. This program, named Daystar, now serves fifteen people each day. And then there's the wellness program at nearby churches I mentioned earlier. From an idea that excited people, a plan was formulated, YMCA staff proactively met with church staff and members, and a ministry outside the YMCA walls was born.

Lest we think that these proactive efforts are limited to large endeavors involving multiple people, I'll share a story about a single YMCA employee who makes a big difference. This lady has a God-given gift for encouragement, which she uses on a regular basis when communicating with fellow employees. Sometimes it's a copy of a devotional or an article waiting on your desk when you arrive at your office. Other times it's a personal note or e-mail. Another day it may be an adage or a Bible verse e-mailed to a group of employees. It is personalized and specific, and though it's not a part of a written, strategic plan, it's still a very intentional effort to reach out to other people and make a difference in their lives. And it does.

No matter where you work, at a YMCA or otherwise, your normal daily activity brings you into contact with a number of people. If you're intentional about it, you can order your days in a way that ensures that you have untold opportunities to encounter people who need something you have. Their need may be as simple as a smile, a hug, or a kind word. Their need may be so complex that it inspires you to organize a group of people, put a structured program together, find resources, and launch a formal ministry. Most of our efforts will be in the middle ground.

I encourage you to not simply *hope* these things happen and that good intentions will somehow magically turn into actions producing good works. Rather, by regularly finding moments of quiet reflection, we avoid staying full speed on the treadmill of life, and can instead be more focused on guiding our lives down the path God has put in front of us. In our reflection times, we can allow God to bring to our minds and hearts the people in our lives that are there for His purpose and whom we have the opportunity to serve daily. By keeping our minds open and our hearts soft to God's leading, we can be aware of not only who to serve but also how to serve them. And finally, as God leads us, we can often bring some planning and structure to our serving. That way, we can ensure that it is done in an organized way, so we can follow through on our good intentions with actions that really do bring God's presence and love with us, no matter where we go or who we're with.

LESSON 10
IN REFLECTION

For Yourself

1. Jesus challenged us to be servants to others. In the last twenty-four hours, describe how you served someone.
2. Have you ever done a secret service or given a gift to someone outside of your normal relationships or in an unexpected setting? What prompted you to do so? How did it make you feel?
3. List the names of five people you can serve this week. How will your service to them meet the needs of the moment?

For Group Discussion and Leadership

1. Consider the foundation and priorities for your organization discussed in Lessons 1 and 9. How do these translate into serving others?
2. Establishing programs or partnerships outside of your own facilities could really serve people in need, but could also generate challenges. Would it be worth the difficulty?
3. Create a long list of opportunities for your organization to serve the community.
4. When was the last time you spent the day in service to others and never entered your office? How did you feel at the end of that day?

11

Small Groups Are
of Great Value

*Christ sent them out "two by two." At one time, he had
five disciples, at another time three, another time
eleven, and at another, twelve. Why did Christ attach
importance to small groups? I long ago decided that
it was wise to follow Christ in this method.*

JRM

by David Byrd

Pretty much every day, it was there: a vodka bottle in
the trash can, a symbol that someone needed help. The
bottles appeared at one of the YMCA facilities in an
affluent part of the city, and we'd find them at night as
we cleaned up.

Initially, because of the regularity, we thought it might
be a staff problem. But we later discovered it was one of
our members, a woman who would come into the facility
at about ten in the morning and stay until midafternoon,
drinking the entire time. It was her escape.

But here's where her story changed. Once we figured
out who she was, we introduced her to Restore
Ministries, a local YMCA program that offers spiritual
and mental healing in small-group settings. That woman
is now in recovery.

She didn't need someone telling her what to do—or
what not to. She needed a close circle of people around
her who would support her, encourage her, and help
her through.

YMCAs and other organizations can be vast institu-
tions, with hundreds on the payroll and thousands of

community members coming through our doors. But to truly reach people where they are, we have to bring it down to a smaller scale. And small groups can be an excellent way of meeting needs—not to mention carrying out the Great Commission.

The Greater Cause

John R. Mott understood that small groups could be one of the pathways to the greater cause of proclaiming the gospel. He believed everyone had an obligation to share Christ with a dislocated society. He said, "It hardly seems right to call a thing impossible or impracticable which has not been attempted. David Livingstone said, 'You don't know what you can do until you try.' The world-wide proclamation of the gospel awaits accomplishment by a generation which shall have the obedience, the courage, and the determination to attempt the task." This is the Mott legacy.

> **"The experience of Christ and those who have most** closely followed Him shows the wisdom of uniting in small bands those who would acquire greatest skill in this highly multiplying work. He not only sent workers out two by two but Himself likewise utilized the group method."[1]   **JRM**

Wherever two or more gather in His name, according to Matthew 18:20, Christ is present. And this is why a small group, formally organized or not, is so important. We need Christ, and we need each other. We need a place to connect. It reminds us that we are not alone. As it says in Hebrews 10:25, we should not be "forsaking our own assembling together," but rather we should be "encouraging one another . . ." (NASB).

Mott believed that this was the ultimate goal of every small group in a church or Christian organization. He said, "There is need throughout all our churches and such bodies as the Young Men's Christian Association of a return to the method of an earlier generation . . . in which small, select groups banded themselves together to train themselves for the vital task of winning others one by one to Christ by studying the Bible in direct preparation for such work and sharing personal insight and experience in the pathway of their services."

The Stories of Our Lives

Mott's small-group philosophy is more than just a good idea. The way I see it, small groups are critical to the mission of the Y. It's still, without a doubt, wise to follow Christ in this method as we set about the life-changing work of ministry.

Small groups bring the story of our lives to others. It's what Frederick Buechner calls "listening to our lives." He writes, "What I propose to do now is to try listening to my life as a whole, or at least to certain key moments of the first half of my life thus far, for whatever of meaning, of holiness, of God, there may be in it to hear. My assumption is that the story of any one of us is in some measure the story of us all." When we read about Peter, James, and John, we can hear in some measure the story of us all. And what we ultimately hear is the story of how Christ fashioned His ministry upon the hinges of small-group dynamics. He banded together a group of misfits that delivered the gospel to their generation. His disciples learned to pray, to heal, to deny themselves, to minister to others.

They also learned what it meant to be human while trying to become Christlike. Peter, James, and John slept through one of the only times Jesus asked for anything. He wanted them to watch and pray; they did neither. When Jesus woke them, they had to feel the poignancy of their failure. At other times, they failed to heal people. James and John's mother went to Jesus to ask for seats on the "right and left" for her sons. When the other disciples learned of this, they were furious (Mark 10:41).

These were not perfect men. They constantly argued about who was going to be the greatest in God's Kingdom. This is why Jesus washed their feet. He wanted them to become servants. Every small group should be a crucible where servanthood is forged.

Building Support

I thoroughly believe that the Y is for everyone, no matter where they live or what their ability to pay. But that takes the generosity of our community. We have a small group of runners who call themselves "Penny Angels" that chips in by collecting coins. As dawn pales the sky, the faint sounds of their running shoes against the downtown sidewalk are overtaken by cries of "penny!" They meet at 5:30 each morning to run and to look for lost coins people have left behind. And over the past fifteen years, those found coins—and occasional bills—have added up to more than twelve hundred dollars for the Y's Youth Development and Y-CAP outreach programs. At the end of each run, the group says a brief prayer asking God to bless America and the other runners. Larry Yarborough, one of the team, says, "We care about each other and about helping the Y reach out to those in need. We really are a family."

We are at our best when we all work together with one unified spirit for the greatest cause.

A Place to Connect

It's no secret that the YMCA helps people live healthier lives. Since our founding in 1875, health-and-wellness programs have been integral to our mission of helping people grow in spirit, mind, and body. Good health is paramount, and small-group settings often provide the context for it.

At our Y, we hold lobby gatherings, where we provide comfortable seating where members can congregate, develop friendships, and talk about real issues in their lives. We want to help people connect, because for some people, it's tempting to go through life never allowing anyone to see behind the facade. This is what bothered Jesus about the Pharisees. As it tells us in Matthew 23:27, He said, "You are like whitewashed tombs which on the outside appear beautiful, but inside they are full of dead men's bones and all uncleanness" (NASB).

Lobby gatherings, support groups, and group-fitness classes can encourage people to relate beneath the surface. Finding a group of people we can "do life" with allows us to unite with a greater power—the presence of Christ. It's just another reason why small groups are so vital. They foster spiritual growth and life-giving connections.

Going Deeper

Small groups can also provide places for confession and healing. Consider the apostle Peter; he'd denied Jesus three times. The rooster crowed in the third watch of Peter's dark night of the soul. It was somewhere between midnight and 3 A.M., somewhere between the person he wanted to be, but didn't have the courage to become. It was cold—cold enough to see your breath—as Peter approached a woman standing with her hands stretched over a fire, as if she were bewitching it. She looked at him closely with the fire reflecting in her eyes and said, "You too were with Jesus, the Galilean," but Peter denied it (Matt. 26:69–70).

At times, we find it easy to deny as well. In general, when someone inquires about our well-being, it's easy to say, "Everything is fine." The intimacy and safety of a small group can give us a place to confess that no, everything really isn't fine. We need confession time, as confession is the one true and holy thing we utter: "Yes, I'm one of them. I believe in spite of my unbelief."

I mentioned Restore Ministries earlier; it's a core outreach program of our Y. Started in 2000, Restore's Christ-centered courses include "Power to Choose," a modified twelve-step process, and "Love is a Choice," a study of codependency and relationship issues.

Regardless of the participant's issue, Restore's programs bring about healing. Scott Reall, who founded the program, attributes that directly to the small-group structure. "The relationships formed are responsible for the healing," he says. "Each group operates on accountability, support, encouragement, and love. All of these are important components of the process."

Benefits from these small groups are dramatic. In addition to developing a general sense of peace, participants have been able to establish boundaries, overcome obsessions, improve relationships, regain hope, and grow stronger in spirit. There are hundreds of stories of healing . . . like the young mother who overcame a crack cocaine addiction and regained custody of her children. A middle-aged man addicted to Internet pornography whose marriage was saved as he went through the program. Today, he is free of this addiction. A suicidal woman who overcame depression and developed a successful career. Restore staff have served as ministers in times of crisis, such as the tragic morning that a young YMCA camp counselor was killed in an auto accident.

> "One of the most intensive methods of liberating the hidden powers of laymen is that of fostering among them the formation of small groups of kindred spirits with an unselfish or service objective. . . . This seems to have been a means through which God during the centuries has accomplished some of His great designs."[2] **JRM**

These small groups also provide a way for participants to maintain their recovery by giving back. Following the initial class, many people increase their involvement with Restore by becoming small-group facilitators, serving on boards, working on committees, or assisting in fund-raising.

In addition, the involvement of churches and group participants has created a strong base of supporters who are aware of the YMCA's commitment to the spiritual, mental, and physical health of individuals in the community.

Sources of Strength

It's a lonely world. And for many, it's only become lonelier in recent years. Our society seems to have lost the art of true communication. We've moved toward personal achievements and performance and have become all too good at having relationships with our computers or televisions rather than with other individuals.

But if we stop to look around us, we'll find ourselves surrounded by people who need someone else in their lives. In the company of others—especially other Christians—we find strength. As we're told in Ecclesiastes 4:12 (NLT), "A person standing alone can be attacked and defeated, but two can stand back-to-back and conquer. Three are even better, for a triple braided cord is not easily broken."

Mott believed that every generation bore this responsibility. He said, "We are responsible for the present generation, that is, for those who are living at the same time as ourselves."

That includes teens and youth. Our YMCA, for example, offers Warren's House, a group home for troubled boys ages twelve to eighteen. Through the program, the boys have a chance to connect in a healthy environment; the small-group setting also provides much-needed direction, support, encouragement, discipline, and spiritual growth.

Pathways For Evangelism

Of course, those young boys aren't the only ones who need help, or the benefits of a small group. There are as many hurting hearts inside an organization as there are outside. And if we don't reach out to them, they will be like a vapor, a part of a lost generation. The psalmist said, "Even when I am old and gray,

O God, do not forsake me, until I declare Your strength to this generation, Your power to all who are to come" (Ps. 71:18 NASB). The psalmist longed to give his testimony to the next generation, and so must we. We must leave behind a furtherance of the Mott legacy by developing strong staff and volunteer leadership. We want to make a positive difference in future generations.

So what does that mean on a practical level? It means offering the possibility of a changed life. Small groups have the potential to impact people in ways that individuals—or large groups—cannot. I'd like to say here, though, that as you pray and seek God's wisdom for the small groups you might offer in your own organization, you keep in mind that at the heart of every small group is the right person leading it. Those who lead should be able to encourage, listen, and build consensus. They must avoid judgmentalism, be able to inspire, and have vision for something that's bigger than themselves.

And they must be willing to hold Mott's legacy in their hands.

> **"Let each one of us join in these groups heartily** and do all in our power to encourage our comrades to do likewise."[3]   **JRM**

As Mott reminds us, the Great Commission is our call. We have to equip not only body and mind, but also spirit. This will take dedicated leaders who are willing to become servants of all. The rich will serve the poor. The stouthearted will heal the brokenhearted. We need leaders who will foster peace and goodwill.

In Mott's "Sam P. Jones Lecture" at Emory University in Atlanta in 1944, he said, "As we go out under the silent heavens looking at the great stars of God, may they teach their lesson, and may these and the example of our Lord continue to speak to us and lead us out into a life of unselfish service to win individuals to Him!"

With small groups that offer strength in numbers, encouragement, places to connect, and even spiritual and emotional healing, YMCAs can only grow stronger. There is, after all, no experience more profound than to gather with two or more in Christ's name, and in the midst of such a gathering, to sense His transforming presence and power.

LESSON 11
IN REFLECTION

For Yourself

1. Why do you suppose Jesus sent out His disciples in pairs? What does that tell you about relationships?
2. Where do you go for connecting and healing? Do you participate in a small group that nurtures you?
3. What are some of the challenges to participating in a small group?
4. If you aren't in a small group—informally or formally structured—where can you go to participate in one?

For Group Discussion and Leadership

1. How does your organization foster small groups among:
   - staff
   - constituents or members
   - volunteers
2. What priority of your organization would be best served by the involvement of small groups?
3. Share a story of how people in your organization connect through small groups.

12

Adolescence Is a Crucial Time

*If I had my life to live over I would spend much time
on the adolescents' age group. These are the habit
forming years, the years of determining life attitude
and tendencies, the years of creativeness.*

JRM

by Wesley Bender
with contributions by Jack Bender

During my last two years of high school, my father
and I really butted heads. I kept procrastinating when it
came to filling out college applications, and my father,
Jack, who was very scheduled and "process-oriented,"
was going crazy. He wanted to make sure everything was
being done in a nice, orderly manner, but I just wanted
to enjoy myself and put it off until later.

We simply couldn't come to terms, and this went on
for awhile. Awhile, that is, until my father had a revelation. He came and sat down with me one day and
admitted that part of the reason he was so upset with me
is that he really didn't want me to go. He wanted me to
go to college, of course, but he wasn't yet ready for me
to leave. He told me he thought that, somehow, I'd
always be around.

Through that talk, the situation changed. We were
able to meet in the middle, and we realized how much
love there was between us and what good friends we had
become. And God made a point of contact, a key connection among people that has meaning and revelation,
that allowed it to happen.

If only we could see all things so clearly. If only we could look at the people around us—yes, even the teenagers who could drive us crazy—and see what's really going on.

In some ways, I believe we can. I believe, with God's help, our eyes can be opened. And we can be newly inspired by what He allows us to see.

Making a Point

Have you ever had a "point of contact" moment yourself? It's one of those times when you realize that there's something much more significant going on than anyone else would have you believe. Our wise predecessor, John R. Mott, had one on January 12, 1886, when he read a Scripture that changed his life. That night at Cornell University, Mott knelt down with his roommate and read Daniel 12:3: "They that be wise shall shine as the brightness of the firmament; and they that turn many to righteousness as the stars forever and ever" (KJV). God made a point of contact with Mott through His Word; for some reason that day, that particular message hit home and made sense to whatever was going on inside of him.

Later in life, I believe Mott had another point of contact. Looking back over his many years, despite his grand accomplishments, he had a revelation. He admitted that with his life to live over, he would do it differently. He would spend more time with adolescents.

I can almost hear you now. "*Adolescents?!*" Yes. Mott believed these years were the ones that determined "life attitude and tendencies, the years of creativeness." Let's be honest. Isn't it all too easy to write teens off as difficult or disinterested? Isn't it too easy to allow them to intimidate us because they're smarter than we really want them to be, and we still want to parent them and guide them in a way they're suddenly no longer comfortable with?

Well, yes. But if we can take Mott's words to heart, we can offer them points of contact that can literally change their lives.

Society's Influence

Okay, so Mott lived a long time ago. Let's have a look at how teenagers are seen today:

Never lend your car to anyone to whom you have given birth.—Erma Bombeck

Adolescence is perhaps nature's way of preparing parents to welcome the empty nest.—Karen Savage and Patricia Adams

Mother Nature is providential. She gives us twelve years to develop a love for our children before turning them into teenagers.—William Galvin

The invention of the teenager was a mistake. Once you identify a period of life in which people get to stay out late but don't have to pay taxes—naturally, no one wants to live any other way.—Judith Martin

There is nothing wrong with today's teenagers that twenty years won't cure.—Author Unknown

The young always have the same problem—how to rebel and conform at the same time. They have now solved this by defying their parents and copying one another.—Quentin Crisp

No doubt about it, teenagers today have been given a bad rap. We too often think that if we can just get them through this time without them getting into any serious trouble, then they can have a positive impact on society. Yet the way Mott put it, quoting another in his book *Five Decades and a Forward View*, "It is a holy sight to see a nation saved by its youth." Mott believed youth wasn't a time to simply be waited out, but a time to fully take advantage.

Today's youth are being pulled at from many angles. Consider what Bob Pittman, the founding chairman of

113

Music Television (MTV), said when the network was initiated: "What we've introduced with MTV is nonnarrative form. . . . We rely on mood and emotion. We make you feel a certain way as opposed to you walking away with any particular knowledge." Any MTV show is strictly geared toward pulling the audience in by tugging at feeling and emotion just to get attention; there is nothing truly beneficial. The results are obvious: the generation that was first introduced to MTV is now the adult generation that cannot get enough reality television—where, unfortunately, usually character doesn't matter and winning at any cost is the goal. (Can you say *Survivor?*)

There are certainly people out there who want to spend time on youth and adolescence; unfortunately, their motives often consist of profit margins and ratings. As the media invades teenagers' development, it teaches them one thing: the less we seek for some definitive purpose for our lives, or some deeper meaning, the closer we are to being "fine" (as the Indigo girls sing in "Closer to Fine"). And that's the most serious problem of all. The less we seek after truth for our lives, the less responsibility we have for ourselves and others, the less we have to worry about our integrity and what we do behind closed doors. We begin to say, in essence, that whatever you do is fine for you as long as it doesn't get in the way of what I want. You do it your way and I'll do it mine, and the only common ground we'll have is that we don't have common ground.

"They are in the habit-forming years, the vision-forming period, the days of great decisions, the time of determining life's attitudes and tendencies. Moreover youth abounds in the spirit of adventure and is responsive to great unselfish challenges."[1]   JRM

We can't entirely blame the media for our sorry state of affairs. A lack of strong moral and ethical values within the family, simple peer influence, and the culture in which teens are reared can all contribute to the problem. Perhaps a big problem is that we don't give teens enough credit or recognize their worth.

Have you ever had to ask your son, daughter, or the neighborhood kid how to work something on your computer, how to save to CD, how to back up a new Palm Pilot, or perhaps how to tape one show while watching another? In a world where kids can sit down to a video game and compete against someone in Japan while talking to him via headset, we quickly realize that today's teenagers do not represent what is wrong with the world; they represent the most intellectual, sophisticated, and creative minds on the planet. John R. Mott believed this and believed all they needed were a few more people to encourage them to be invested in the common mission of unity in Christ. The end result is that every generation of youth could be challenged with the meaning and purpose that is found in giving back to others their talents, learning about themselves, and having faith.

Finding a Strategy

Personally, I was fortunate to grow up in a family that was close, a place where we could all laugh with each other, have fun, and be genuine. As a matter of fact, it's still that way, and my father has had a great hand in helping me write this chapter.

But working with youth, I've come to discover that a lot of them didn't have that. And I just can't stand the idea that these kids have to go home to places that are not full of joy, and instead live in places where they feel scared or that they have to hide things. I know, then, that that's one of the things God has personally called me to do: to help provide a joyful, safe environment where teens can go to find love and fellowship with others. At the same time, I've discovered that there's nothing I can really do to change a teen. All I can do is give them positive end results to work toward, allow them to get caught up in the case, and help them be in the right place at the right time so it becomes a godly point of contact.

Sometimes God uses the most difficult times to make a point of contact with us. That could mean a near-death experience, the death of a close friend, a son who just won't get his act straight, or a time that you seem to have so much on your shoulders that you feel you have no place to turn. But sometimes He uses the most joyful periods, such as the birth of a child, or graduation, or even a wedding. Whenever it may be, the premise is that God is always struggling to pull us away from the television, the video game, the movie, or maybe even all those good deeds we do simply to tell us He loves us. God offers a simple gesture in order that He might make a connection with us.

Let's look at an example from a man who knew full well what it meant for God to make a point of contact with him. In Acts 9, a man named Paul (through a very large interaction with God) went from persecuting Jesus to proclaiming His love and grace and mercy to all. From there, he began using the same idea to make a point of contact with other people to spread the gospel.

Paul had to build respect with people in three different cities. While in Thessalonica, Paul went first to the synagogue, as was the Jewish custom. There he interpreted the Scriptures to the people. The people in Thessalonica were predominantly Jewish, so Paul first showed his knowledge of the ancient texts and then showed his agreement with the importance of the synagogue. As Paul pulled them in using this familiarity, he then gained their respect and could share the Good News of Jesus.

Next, we find Paul in Berea, where he met with intellectual Jewish leaders who tested his knowledge. Paul was able to connect with this group by proclaiming his extensive knowledge of the Scriptures. "As a result," it says in Acts 17:12, "many Jews believed, as did some of the prominent Greek women and many men" (NLT). Finally, Paul ministered in Athens. He knew little about the culture and people there, but through the statue of the Unknown God, he was able to make a point of contact with them regardless, going on to share the Good News. In order for people to genuinely see the truth and take hold of it in their lives, they must first be allowed to make a point of contact that they can relate to.

Seeking Purpose

Human nature usually steers us toward discovering things for ourselves rather than being told a bunch of rules and regulations on how to live our lives. That's especially true with teens, it seems. For this reason, the point of contact that God makes with each of us is very different. There is no outline or book that takes everyone step by step to a lasting relationship, and there are certainly no seven guiding principles to finding our purpose in this life.

I was caught off guard one evening after a meeting with about sixty high school teenagers of all different cultures, races, and religions. The meeting was a three-hour workshop, and we were hoping to find fifteen strong leaders who would help us open a new state-of-the-art YMCA teen facility in Alpharetta, Georgia. We had tons of group work, team building exercises, and discussions. I talked about the new facility and how it had an Internet radio station, a concert area, speakers, and all kinds of other amenities. After the meeting, one young man opened the door to a conversation I'll never forget. He was a stereotypical teenager: tall and skinny, with long hair that covered his eyes, and he looked as if he were going to put his headphones on as soon as he walked out the door.

He was shaking and shuffling his papers as he asked, "Mr. Wes, at this teen center, are we going to be able to play music like you would hear on the radio . . . you know, music that is a little more secular with cuss words and stuff?" The whole concept of the Teen Center is that it is completely student-led, so I simply reversed the question. I said, "Well, that's one of the things that this board of fifteen we're choosing will have to decide. What do you think?"

William, the teenager, hesitated for just a second and then said, "I don't think we should." Honestly, I was a little surprised, so I asked him why not. It wasn't the fact that he answered with, "Because it does not promote morals and ethics and values we want our generation to represent," that startled me the most. It was the fact that, when I asked him where he went to church, he said, "I have never been to church." Talk about a kick in the pants.

This kid knew right from wrong. He even knew good virtues. The extent of what I could tell him was already over. What he needed was a point of contact with the God that gave all of his knowledge meaning. There are thousands of youth organizations out there who can tell kids right from wrong and what they should and should not do. There are some dynamite trainings geared toward equipping teenagers with what they need to succeed. However, if we do not battle the problem of getting kids to seek after the truth in life through a personal interaction or point of contact with God, all we've done is given them a bigger house with a fancier car.

As for John R. Mott, his Student Volunteer Movement had a singular purpose. It wasn't so much for the "Christianization" of the world. Instead, it was that every person of that generation would have an opportunity to accept Jesus Christ. How can we not be compelled to do the same?

Looking for Something Better

At this point, it's probably easy to see where my father and I fit into the Christian mission of the YMCA. We feel very strongly about it. On the flip side, we also believe that the YMCA is not the church and shouldn't function as the church should function. The question, then, is what *should* our path be in fulfilling our Christian mission with teenagers? Again, I believe that the YMCA should create arenas that allow God to make points of contact with people, namely teens. We're not the ones who change people's hearts or even get them to agree with our opinions. Our duty is to create situations away from the negative influences of society so that God can meet kids who are ready. To make it happen, we also must develop a core network of strong volunteers who are committed to being mentors, committed to the call, and willing to overcome the challenges.

In 2 Timothy 1:5-8, Paul wrote to Timothy:

> I know that you sincerely trust the Lord, for you have the faith of your mother, Eunice, and your grandmother, Lois. This is why I remind you to fan into flames the spiritual gift God gave you when I laid my hands on you. For God has not given us a spirit of fear and timidity, but of power, love, and self-discipline. So you must never be ashamed to tell others about our Lord. And don't be ashamed of me, either, even though I'm in prison for Christ. With the strength God gives you, be ready to suffer with me for the proclamation of the Good News (NLT).

In this passage, Paul demonstrates two great principles. First, he talks about the tradition of generations. If we teach today's teenagers to seek after something better, it has a trickle-down effect to the generations after them. Second, by giving youth the gift of seeking after purpose, we are in essence doing away with fear and timidity. We, instead, allow them to develop power, love, self-discipline, and unselfish behaviors. We also allow them to understand the talents God has given them and

"**Great is the need of a leadership which has the** priceless gift of appreciation of youth and sympathy with youth. The men and women with this gift . . . exercise an influence which reaches into the second and even the third generation."[2]   **JRM**

to use those talents in service to others. We're doing much more than equipping them; we are allowing them to equip themselves. Radical? Absolutely. Impossible? Absolutely not. I've seen it many times: give a kid everything he needs to make a decision, and nine times out of ten, he'll make the right one. The hardest part is often mustering up our own faith that God will help.

God's Promise to Help

But it's God's very pledge to us: for anyone who seeks after truth, for anyone who seeks after meaning, definition, or a purpose for life, He meets that person right where they are. Listen to these promises:

> And he will give you all you need from day to day if you live for him and make the Kingdom of God your primary concern (Matt. 6:33 NLT).

> Keep on asking, and you will be given what you ask for. Keep on looking and you will find. Keep on knocking, and the door will be opened. For everyone who asks, receives. Everyone who seeks, finds. And the door is opened to everyone who knocks (Matt. 7:7–8 NLT).

> Salvation has come to this home today, for this man has shown himself to be a son of Abraham. And I, the Son of Man, have come to seek and save those like him who are lost (Luke 19:9–10 NLT).

> So, you see, it is impossible to please God without faith. Anyone who wants to come to him must believe that there is a God and that he rewards those who sincerely seek him (Heb. 11:6 NLT).

> Now to him who by the power at work within us is able to do more than all we can ask or imagine . . . (Eph. 3:20 NRSV).

Mott wrote that if a man was drowning in a lake because he couldn't swim, Confucius would tell the man to profit by his experience. A follower of Buddhism might simply say, "Struggle." A Hindu person might tell the man to look for his opportunity in the next incarnation. Muhammad would believe, whether or not the man was saved or not, that it was the will of God. But Jesus and His followers would reach out their hands and meet the man right where he was and pull him out of the lake.

We cannot pull people into Christianity, but we certainly can be the vessels God uses to pull them out of whatever trials they are experiencing. If that means creating environments that are safe and away from the influences we have talked about, or if it means creating a support group for people with similar needs, it all leads them to a place where God can make a point of contact with them. In this way, we, as Christians, are functioning as mere instruments of the grace and mercy of God. We must be idealistic; if we are first faithful to God, so also will be those we serve. "And now, dear brothers and sisters, let me say one more thing as I close this letter. Fix your thoughts on what is true and honorable and right. Think about things that are pure and lovely and admirable. Think about things that are excellent and worthy of praise," it says in Philippians 4:8 (NLT). We must be people of character.

You know what I mean here. Teens are too perceptive for us to be anything other than genuine. And the most important thing, when working with teens, is to work on ourselves first.

Providing What They Need

We must always remember that today's generation of teenagers—and the generations of teenagers to come—will always be elements of change in our world. They represent the present as well as the promise of the future. In these habit-forming years, they are making decisions that change our culture for better or for worse.

How do we give them the principles they need to change the world for the better? We must make sure that the people who guide and work with them are solid in character. We must live strong, powerful, and self-disciplined lives for the Kingdom.

After that, we must recognize that our popular culture discourages teens from seeking after definition, purpose, and truth for their lives. We must grasp the

> **"This ministry of sharing with others the deepest** things of life—even the knowledge of Christ Himself—constitutes the highest office of friendship. It is the work to-day [sic] most needed, the most highly multiplying, the most enduring, the most apostolic, the most truly Christlike and, therefore, incomparably the most important."[3]   **JRM**

premise that God is constantly trying to offer His love, grace, and mercy through points of contact. We must create the path of programming in our organizations for strong mentors and arenas in which God can work. And we must have faith that He will come through. We can start with Romans 12:2:

> Don't copy the behavior and customs of this world, but let God transform you into a new person by changing the way you think. Then you will know what God wants you to do and you will know how good and pleasing and perfect his will really is (NLT).

In the end, you can be the point of contact leading to the prayer of Jesus, "that they may all be one. As you, Father, are in me and I am in you," as it reads in John 17:21, "may they also be in us, so that the world may believe that you have sent me" (NRSV).

LESSON 12
IN REFLECTION

For Yourself

1. Think back to when you were a teenager. What crucial lessons did you learn about purpose and truth for your life?
2. How do those life lessons affect your walk with God today?
3. How have you supported a young person in making a point of contact with God?

For Group Discussion and Leadership

1. Organizations go through phases of maturity. Describe what the "adolescent" stage of an organization would look like.
2. What stage is your organization in? What crucial lessons has your organization learned during its adolescent stage?
3. How does your organization seek definition, purpose, and truth?
4. Discuss how you can create strong mentors and arenas for adolescents in which God can make a point of contact.

13

Don't Overlook Old People

Here is wisdom and experience for our asking.
Here, also, is a group to whom we must
give kindness and affection.
JRM

by Burnie Whitson

2,174 miles! For more than two decades, this number keeps finding its way to the front of my brain, only to be pushed back with a promise of, "Later." I am now in the shadows of the half-century mark in age, and I still have not made the time to deal with those miles. Oh, I've dealt with them in my mind, but my imagination is where they have stayed.

The Appalachian Trail begins its path in northern Georgia, climbing as high as 6,625 feet at Clingman's Dome in North Carolina, and ends 2,174 miles later at Mount Katahdin, Maine. And my dream has been to become a member of the 2,000-mile club, a prestigious group that welcomes only those who have walked the entire length. But I don't just want to walk the trail; I want to experience it. And I don't want to just experience it alone. I want to experience it with my children and even future grandchildren.

This dream is important to me because experiencing the trail is a parallel to my spiritual walk, and it's a vivid reminder of my own mortality. And thanks to a woman named Janet, it has proven to me the wisdom of

John R. Mott's encouragement to embrace the experiences of those who are a few mile markers ahead of us on the trail of life.

Those Who Have Gone Before

It would have been easy to write Janet off and see her as just some older woman. But what simple wisdom she possessed by virtue of her experience! She had done things I hadn't. She'd done things I only dreamed of. And, if I listened carefully to her wisdom, what mistakes she could help me prevent!

I first met Janet in late 1982. I was a young fitness director for the YMCA, and she was a new member who really didn't need the Y for exercise. She joined so that her husband might start working out. Janet was already in her late forties, which seems young to me today. But at the time, she seemed past her prime. Janet faithfully came to the YMCA for many more years, even though her husband lost interest in the whole exercise idea after about a year. Through those years, she shared pieces of her life with me. I discovered that she was a nurse and an avid swimmer, she loved to square dance, and she took great pride in teaching CPR for the Red Cross. She was the quintessential grandmother for the '90s. But, alas, other things began to battle for her time, and she stopped coming to the YMCA. It would be at least five years before we crossed paths again.

On a warm spring Tuesday, I rushed into my one o'clock Rotary Club meeting five minutes late and quickly grabbed a salad before the president's gavel banged to signal the lowering of our forks. When I looked to the podium, I saw Janet sitting at the guest speaker's spot. I assumed that Janet was there to share about a community event sponsored by the Red Cross or about some mission effort of her church. Boy, was I surprised when the Rotarian who was introducing her reached down and picked up a twenty-five-pound backpack and placed it on the table beside the podium. He said, "Today we will hear from a sixty-five-year-old grandmother who just completed hiking the two-thousand-plus miles of the Appalachian Trail." I had jumped to the wrong conclusion, putting Janet in the cloak of a grandmother when she truly deserved a spot as the newest member in my hall of fame.

The first thing that Janet said was, "If you want to hike the AT, then you must be properly prepared." In my mind, I began assembling a list of what I needed to do to hike the trail: *Be prepared.* Janet then unpacked her pack and showed us her bedroll, tent, cooking set, food, change of clothes, water purification kit, and trail maps. Throughout her talk, I was picking up tidbits to accomplish my dream, guided along the way by someone who had been there. *Don't pack too much. Wear the right kind of shoes.*

Sitting in that room hearing from someone else who had lived my dream, God began to show me how walking the AT was like our spiritual walk with Him. He has clearly marked the path that our Lord Jesus Christ walked for us. His words will help us finish our lives strong no matter what age we might be. And He has put people on the path who are a few steps ahead. If we listen to their wisdom, we can avoid the rocks along the path and find the most amazing spots to view sunsets.

Honoring the Accomplishments of Others

By the year 2020, the U.S. Census Bureau believes that the population of people aged sixty-five and older will have grown from the current 34 million to 53 million. As for those aged eighty-five and older, the Census Bureau forecasts a doubling from 3.5 million to 7 million people.

In the YMCA, we talk often about this growing senior population. We've created fitness classes just for them called "Silver Sneakers" and social clubs called "Silver Foxes." Financial analysts speak about the great transfer of wealth that will take place as these baby boomers age into their senior years. Nonprofit organizations like the YMCA and churches are eager to recruit these seniors as volunteers. But how often do we ask these seniors, who have walked all of their lives with God, for their wisdom? Yes, their money and their time are valuable to us, but we don't want to ask them what they think. The writer of Proverbs says, "The silver-haired head is a crown of glory, if it is found in the way of righteousness" (16:31 NKJV).

John R. Mott said, "Religious truth was not intended merely to be contemplated; it was designed to be done. Our moral and religious life is not a train of thoughts but a life of action, of constant exertion of the will." Mott led that life of action as he continuously put feet to the gospel of Jesus Christ. In 1946, John R. Mott was awarded the Nobel Peace Prize at the age of eighty-one. Herman Smitt Ingebretsen said this about Mott in his presentation speech at the Nobel Institute: "His work has always been chiefly among youth, for in them lies the key to the future. They are the leaders of tomorrow. The spirit that moves the hearts of young will one day fashion the world. And the old John Mott is still to be found in the midst of the young, a tireless servant of his Master."

The one thing that I fear about growing old is having no purpose. Our culture has changed through the years from respecting and honoring our elders to ignoring the wisdom that they have acquired through their walk.

My dad is eighty-three years old, and I realize that I don't ask him for his wisdom often enough. I know that he and Mom raised me to be an independent thinker and that they made sure I was well grounded in God's Word. But I now realize that I don't want to be eighty-three and have my kids not ask my opinion anymore. God grant me—and all of us—forgiveness for forgetting how to honor our elders. Engrave on our hearts: *"You shall rise before the gray headed and honor the presence of an old man"* (Lev. 19:32 NKJV).

And so, as soon as that Rotary meeting was over, I rushed to the front to greet Janet and to tell her how inspired I was over her accomplishment. She explained how she started out taking short day hikes locally and eventually began to tackle sections of the AT. She began doing just a couple of days and then warmed up to stints of more than a week on the trail. It had taken her almost a decade to complete her journey.

Now, all the time that she was talking, I couldn't get that 2,174 number pushed to the back of my head. I had tremendous respect for what she had accomplished, but I was also thinking that if she didn't start until her early fifties and was still hiking in her mid-sixties, then my unrealized dream was not yet dead. Maybe I could still hike the entire trail. Janet had inspired me and had rekindled my dream, but would I be so bold and ask her to teach me?

Before I could ask, Janet said, "Would you like to borrow my trail guides and my personal journal that I kept?" I could hardly contain myself. It was as if she had said, "Here, look into my soul and see what I was experiencing."

Before she could change her mind, I said yes, and I promised to protect and cherish her documents while they were in my possession.

Leaving the Trail Ready

I loved reading Janet's journals. I felt many times as if I were on the trail. But I also wondered, after one accomplishes such a task, do you dream of doing it again? So I asked Janet, "Do you think that you will hike the trail again, or has the experience lost its luster?" Janet said, "I'm going this weekend to help repair a section of the trail." She went on to explain that she was a member of a Trail Club. Club members are assigned a section of the trail that they are responsible for maintaining. They repaint the blazes on the trees and rocks to mark the trail. They also clean the shelters and privies and pack out trash that hikers leave behind. In the spring, they cut back weeds, lop off low-hanging branches, and clean up blown down trees after storms.

Janet said, "I like helping keep the trail in good shape so that other hikers can enjoy their experience like I enjoyed mine." Just as I had suspected, my new hero also had the heart of a servant. She knew that we must make the path clear for the next generation.

When I was a young boy, the older men in my church would spend time with me on a baseball field or on a basketball court. It may have seemed like no big deal—just some men hanging out at the basketball court. But I was watching their lives, seeing their authentic walks, which cleared the path for me.

I learned through the experience that it's important to not let the wisdom of older people's walks go unshared. And that's not just on a personal level. At our organizations, we can—and should—ask our senior citizens to volunteer with our youth programs. You could, for example, make the volunteer experience structured so that they share in a storytelling format, or you could just have them share their love by giving their time.

> "To have a knowledge of Jesus Christ is to incur a tremendous responsibility to those that have it not. You and I have received this great heritage, not to appropriate it to our own exclusive use, but to pass it on to others. It concerns all men. We are trustees of the gospel, and in no sense sole proprietors."[1]   **JRM**

It's so important for us to remember that the "Go ye therefore and teach" command has no age restrictions and no time deadlines. Give older people time to share the love of God as trustees of the gospel, and the message of Jesus Christ will be carried to the next generation.

Picking Good Fruit

It was early fall a few years ago, and my dad and I were doing some day hiking at the Peaks of Otter near Bedford,

Virginia. The AT is only about five miles north of the Peaks of Otter. After we had finished our picnic, we loaded up and headed down the mountain. As we wound our way down to civilization, we passed a roadside fruit stand with an apple orchard beside it. I quickly cut a deal for us to pick a bushel and to eat as many as we could while we were picking. I was determined to be selective and find the biggest fruit. Most of the rows had young trees that stretched eight to nine feet in the air and were loaded with apples. On the back row of the orchard stood four trees that stretched twelve to fifteen feet in the air and probably were at least fifty years old. These four patriarchs of the orchard didn't seem to have lured many pickers to their tall branches. Why? Well, the limbs of these trees had a lot less foliage on them and even less fruit compared to their younger counterparts. But each tree had a dozen or more apples scattered throughout its branches. These apples were the best of the crop. You had to work to get them because it was as if each tree put all of its energy into pushing out one big apple on the end of its tallest limbs.

I knew that if I could find the oldest trees then I would also find the best fruit, knowledge gained working on a peach farm as a teen. Picking this type of fruit takes longer, but I know that the effort seems small once you have held that fruit in your hand.

Older people who have walked with God all of their lives also produce the best spiritual fruit. Sometimes we overlook these mature believers because they can't physically keep up with the younger people.

I regret I lost opportunities to listen to the travels that my fellow pilgrims had been on when I was a young officer in the church. What wonderful stories they must have had. What life lessons I could have learned. If I had given them time, I would have avoided some dangers in the paths that I would come to follow them in, and I would have allowed them to remain useful in Kingdom ministry, as well. Give time and respect, and you will reap great wisdom. It's no irony that those who have the least time left on this earth are the ones who seem to know where to best use that time: investing in the lives of others, taking time out for a cup of coffee, allowing their schedules to be changed when someone wants to talk.

We need to remember that we won't be the last of the hikers on the trail of life. There are those behind us who see us as elders, no matter how few gray hairs we may have. If we're willing to share just a bit of our lives with them, we too can help someone find the path. Even if we're just at mile marker number one, there's always someone who has just started to walk.

LESSON 13
IN REFLECTION

For Yourself

1. Who has walked before you that is willing to share wisdom?
2. What do you fear most about growing old?
3. How can you help an older believer continue being a servant leader?
4. Who do you need to encourage to continue producing good fruit?

For Group Discussion and Leadership

1. How does your organization seek the wisdom of past leaders?
2. How does your organization respect and honor past leaders?
3. What in your culture provides encouragement for the older generation of staff and volunteers?
4. Discuss how you may have overlooked mature leaders and believers in your organization. How can they help you leave a legacy for future generations?

14

Emphasize the Immediate

We need to live under the spell of immediacy.
What other time will there be? What other
generations than the present can we work with?
JRM

by Craig Seibert

It's always there, in the same place, a constant reminder to look for God's activity in my life at work. Yes, at work.

You see, I keep a couple of journals. There's one at home in which I reflect on things like my family, my kids, and what God's teaching me through the Scriptures. But there's also one I keep at work, and that's the one that really helps me see how active God is in my daily life. Whenever God shows up during my workday, whenever He interrupts my day in a healthy way and uses me for His purposes, whenever He allows me to minister spiritual truth, or I see Him working behind the scenes, it goes in there. And not only does it encourage me, it helps me show others how God is at work all around us.

In this day and age, what people really want is to experience a living, breathing, real God. And if I have a record to account for the way He's involved in my everyday life, that's so much more than doing the church routine on a Sunday morning. It gives me a fresh reservoir to draw from.

It's too easy to forget the little things that God does for us, isn't it? Even if they seemed miraculous at the time, chances are, if we don't stay aware, those things get crowded out by the busyness of life. But consider Ephesians 5:16. It reminds us to be always "Redeeming the time for the days are evil" (KJV).

In other words, we're responsible for how we invest our time on earth. Now, time is the great equalizer. Everyone has the same amount of it in a twenty-four-hour day. Rich or poor, young or old, tall or short, male or female, and whatever nationality or ethnicity, everyone has the same amount of time. This makes time a very valuable commodity indeed, because every individual has the same opportunity to invest it in making an eternal difference.

But it's not just about setting priorities. There are other questions we must answer. How, for example, can we live with a sense of immediacy? How can we make our lives useful for Kingdom purposes? How can we redeem our time so it counts for eternity?

Those questions are all entwined. If we answer one of them, we have, in effect, answered them all. What makes for an interesting process is to back into the answers to these questions by asking another one: "Why do we not live with a sense of immediacy?"

The Busyness of Life

Let's talk about that busyness of life. It seems like everyone is busy, overcommitted, and overworked. People give a variety of reasons for this: being asked to work more and more hours, kids' schedules, taking care of everyday things, church commitments, and more.

As a response to why we're not living in the immediate, though, it seems counterintuitive. If we're busy and running a mile a minute, aren't we living in the immediate? Aren't we accomplishing a lot?

Well, not necessarily. You may be getting a lot of things done, but are they really the right things?

Rather than being fully present in the moment personally, emotionally, and spiritually, we tend to become a blur without substance. Our bodies are running around frantically driving to work, school, or sports events, but our minds are elsewhere. We're so busy thinking about the ten other things we have to do that we're not fully present.

Compounding this is the pressure we feel to say yes to new and great opportunities, or the chance to do good things. We feel like it's important to be current on sports, trivia, *New York Times* bestsellers, arts, plays, skiing, TV programming, movies, music, technologies, and more. It's exhausting.

Consider this: one Sunday edition of the *New York Times* contains more information than a person would have been exposed to in a lifetime two hundred years ago. We are simply overrun with information, opportunities, and choices.

Even back in 1987, John Oswalt wrote in his book, *The Leisure Crisis:*

> The people in North America and Europe have more discretionary time than they have ever had before (as far as working toward basic needs being met), however it is also true that there are hundreds of unworthy claimants for that time.

The issue of living with a sense of immediacy, then, is about more than managing schedules, to-do lists, and tasks, or even establishing priorities. To deal with the busyness, we have to ask ourselves which things are most important. Which things are worth focusing our lives on?

Preoccupied With the Here and Now

Modern people do not live with a sense of legacy-mindedness. We live with the adrenaline pump of the here and now. What can I do for my next thrill? How can I "be all that I can be"? How can I become known as a person of influence, success, or importance?

Personally, I'm amazed by how quickly famous and successful people are forgotten. John R. Mott is a perfect example. Just fifty years ago, he was the Billy Graham of his time. He was a major player on the world stage. Leaders of churches, other religions, and nations knew his name. He was friend to presidents and statesmen. People involved in the YMCA who love history have kept his name and impact alive, but in general, a household name of just fifty years ago has faded from the minds of the world. And he's not alone.

To further bring this point home, consider this story from the book *Calm My Storm, Lord*.

In 1898, Erasmus Arlington Pond was pitcher with the Baltimore Orioles. His team had won the prestigious Templeton Cup (the precursor to today's World Series) twice in a row, and would win it again that season. Pond's teammates included what are now six Hall of Famers, including John McGraw and Wee Willie Keeler. A medical student at Johns Hopkins at the same time, Pond gave up his baseball career to go to the Philippines as an assistant surgeon in the Spanish-American War.

Once there, Pond was visibly moved by the plight of the natives, and when the war was over, remained there under the auspices of the Rockefeller Foundation as a physician and public health officer, giving up his baseball career entirely to do so.

Pond became one of the more famous Americans in the days after the war, and is credited with implementing procedures and treatments that would eventually dramatically diminish (and in some cases, completely eradicate) the effects of bubonic plague, cholera, leprosy and more. When he died of appendicitis in 1930, the whole nation mourned his loss, as well as his friends President William Howard Taft, Leonard Wood and John McGraw (who had even taken a team of

Yankees over to the Philippines for an exhibition with his old friend and teammate).

Yet when I heard his story, barely a trace of it still existed. His 84-year-old nephew happened to be a neighbor and mentioned it to me one night in passing. It took nearly four years of research to uncover the details described above. But for that brief conversation with his nephew, Pond's story would have disappeared in the bowels of libraries where no one ever goes, a footnote in history no one ever reads.

And if this story about Erasmus Pond does not speak to the fleetingness of fame, fortune, and success even when a life is lived well spent, this poem by Saxon White Kessinger should finalize our view:

Indispensable Man

Sometime when you're feeling important,
Sometime when your ego's in bloom,
And the times when you take it for granted,
You're the best qualified in the room,
Sometime when you feel that your going
Would leave an unfillable hole,
Just follow these simple instructions
And see how it humbles your soul;
Take a bucket and fill it with water,
Put your hand in it up to the wrist,
Pull it out and the hole that's remaining
Is a measure of how you'll be missed.
You may splash all you please when you enter,
You can stir up the water galore,
But stop and you'll find in a minute
That it looks quite the same as before.
The moral of this quaint example
Is do just the best that you can,
Be proud of yourself, but remember,
There's no indispensable man.

Humbling, isn't it? Makes me wonder this: if fame and success are so fleeting, what on earth can we live for that will bring deep satisfaction as we look back on our lives? Well, the things that last for eternity are the only things that will bring this level of satisfaction, and there are three of them: 1) God Himself, 2) His Word, and 3) people. Everything else is left behind.

If we truly believe this, it will guide our choices in making an eternal impact with our lives. Not that relaxing, watching a sitcom, catching a movie, or reading the sports page aren't good things; everyone needs some down time. Yet, how are we doing as far as giving attention to the three things that go on forever?

> **"Our conquest of time is through design, through** choice, through a plan, through system. Every day we should ask ourselves, How can I best spend this day?"[1]
> **JRM**

One way I challenge myself and others is to see how well I do at answering "yes" to some of these questions dealing with God, His Word, and people. As you approach these questions, ask yourself if you're comfortable with the number you can say yes to. And then take it a step further: could you train and equip someone else to say yes to these questions?

- Is your relationship with God fresh?
- Do you feel like God is using you to your maximum ability?
- Do you know how to walk in the daily power of God's spirit?
- Do you have a sense of calling and purpose?
- Are you confident in knowing how to read and understand the Bible for yourself?
- Do you know how to apply biblical principles to life's daily issues?
- Do you know how to lovingly help others apply biblical truth to their lives?

- If God really began to work in people's hearts, and you suddenly had ten people that you had to help grow to spiritual maturity, could you do it?
- Do you have a sense of community with others who are like-minded in their desire to make a Kingdom difference?
- Do you have accountability to make the most of your life and to stay on the right track?
- Are you confident that you could clearly share how God is working in your life or how you came to faith in Christ?
- Are you confident that you could share your faith in such a way that someone else would know how to become a Christian if they wanted to?
- Could you disciple a new believer into spiritual maturity?

Okay, I'm convicted. Are you?

Maybe you're one of those people who feel they have no time in their lives for anything else. And if that's so, it may be time to reevaluate how you spend your time. There may be some things that you want to choose not to do anymore, as well as some things that you want to start doing, things that can make an eternal difference. And cultivating this perspective in thinking will give you a sense of living in the immediate.

Misinformed Perspective

Most of us today live with a teenager's perspective on life: we're simply going to live forever. Death and dying take place on some distant calendar date that will happen eventually, but it seems too far in the future to worry about. But the Bible tells us something different. It tells us that our life is like the morning mist. In truth, it's over very quickly.

Have you ever considered that you're really nothing more than a two-pound dust bunny? If you actually went around the house and reached way back under the beds and in the closets and collected all the dust and put it together and smashed it down, you could be looking down at you. Doctors tell us that, minus the water that makes up 90 percent of our bodies, we're about two pounds of dust.

And yet, the sovereign God of the universe has breathed His life into us and is allowing us to participate in His Kingdom plan to change the world. Unbelievable news, isn't it?

So let's take a closer look at the life of the two-pound dust bunny that lives only as long as the morning mist, and see exactly how much time there is to make an impact.

If you're currently twenty years old and live to an average life expectancy of about seventy-five years, you have about twenty thousand days to invest before you leave this earthly realm. If you're twenty-five, under the same formula, you've got about eighteen thousand days. At thirty-five, the number is fifteen thousand; at forty-five, it's eleven thousand. At fifty-five, it's seven thousand; at sixty-five, it's four thousand, and finally, at age seventy, it's two thousand.

But wait, we're not done yet.

As we mentioned earlier, we're all given the same amount of time each week: 168 hours. How we choose to spend that time is up to us, but statistics show the way a typical week is spent:

- forty-nine hours sleeping
- forty-two hours working
- fifteen hours eating
- ten hours in the car
- seven hours getting ready
- five hours shopping
- four hours on the phone or e-mail
- three hours exercising
- two hours cleaning the house
- two hours waiting for someone else
- two hours in church

This leaves about twenty-seven hours of time that could still be "invested." However, not included on this list are the average fifteen hours of TV each week and five hours of other entertainment that people spend.

So now we're down to seven hours a week. Accounting for other things that come up that take four or five hours a week, only two hours remain.

No wonder people feel they are too busy and exhausted with life. And no wonder the Bible tells us that our life is like the morning mist.

> **"Time is really your life measured out to you for work;** and each successive moment, as Edward Thring said, is actually the end of that bit of available life. So time is, in fact, the measure of the capacity of this life of ours. This, then, is the reason why time should be redeemed, why it is important to use it rightly."[2]   **JRM**

If you'd like to get a better grip on what hours you do have, I'd recommend that this week you take a blank sheet of paper and literally track how you spend your time. If you like, you can do it in thirty-minute increments. Then, at the end of the week, review what you wrote down. How do you spend your time?

Next, take action. What one, two, or three things do you need to stop doing right now that are simply a waste of time or represent time that you really want for something else? What could you do more efficiently to gain more time? And if you do gain more time, will the new things you choose to add allow you to say yes to more of the questions posed in the previous section?

Sacred Versus Secular

If you do the exercise in the previous section, I can almost guarantee it will produce some fruitful results. But let's not stop there. I'd like to address an issue that seems to be the bane of the modern church: the sacred-secular divide.

In our compartmentalized society, we move from one task or activity to another. We have separate compartments for everything.

The sacred-secular divide tells us that some activities (going to church, ministry involvement, Bible study, etc.) are more sacred than other things (work, exercise, hanging out with friends). But this isn't biblical teaching.

If the average person has 168 hours each week and almost 50 hours are used for sleep, there are actually more than 2, 6, or 12 hours that are redeemable for God's Kingdom purposes. How about 118? Work with me here: we can make the mental shift that our every waking moment can be harnessed for God's Kingdom purposes through how we live, think, and make ourselves available. We can be at the point God can show up anywhere and use us, and not just in those six hours a week we carve out for ministry time.

That doesn't mean that we become a people that others have suggested are "so spiritually minded, they are no earthly good." What it does mean, however, is that as we seek to yield ourselves to God, He can interrupt our routine at any time. It might be a thought of someone to pray for on the way to work; a phone call or an e-mail; or an interruption on the job where someone needs a word of encouragement or maybe a word of truth. Maybe someone needs an undistracted ear, or even just some friendship time.

All of this is redeemable time that puts us in the immediacy of living if we are allowing God to make His presence known through us in the here and now.

Unpreparedness

Of course, for God to use us, it'll take more than just a little extra time. We also need to be prepared. As the apostle Peter wrote to first century believers, "Always be prepared to give an answer to everyone who asks you to give the reason for the hope that you have" (1 Pet. 3:15 NIV). And boy, have some of us failed on this challenge. Christians have been called a mile wide and an inch deep. A large number of people consider themselves to be Christians, but the depth of their relationship with God or their ability to share how God has impacted their life or how another person can come to know God is grossly wanting.

> **"The right use of time today creates the great opportunity for tomorrow."**[3] **JRM**

To me, being prepared means being able to share what God has done in my life with clarity and brevity. It means being willing to be interrupted, and seeing that God really does have work for me to do all around me, no matter where I am or who I'm with. It means living with immediacy.

Any time I need a reminder, I get out that workplace journal that I keep in my office. It brings me confidence; it reminds me how God has helped me move around— or even prevent—problems. And it helps me remember that sovereign connection in my everyday life.

The way I see it, if Jesus is within us, that means He goes wherever we go. So, yes, He's there at the office. He's on the basketball court. And He's in the coffee shop when you're meeting with a friend. And all the while, He's there, looking to leak His love out of you—and use you to change eternity.

LESSON 14
IN REFLECTION
For Yourself

1. During the exercise on page 141, what one or two things did you identify that you want to stop doing? How will you put this into action this week?
2. How do your priorities make your life count for Kingdom purposes?
3. How did your actions yesterday count for eternity?

For Group Discussion and Leadership

1. What can you do as a leader of your organization to promote a culture of emphasizing the immediate?
2. How does your ability to live in the present affect those you supervise?
3. God, His Word, and people go on forever. How do your organization's foundation, principles, and priorities reflect this fact?

15

Be Attentive unto God

"Speak Lord, for thy servant hearkens," and
"My soul, be silent unto God" say what I mean.
We must put out other sounds—noises of
selfish ambition—prepare ourselves to say,
"Speak Lord, for thy servant hearkens."

JRM

by W. Tracy Howe

My middle child, Austin, runs high school track. On a beautiful spring day, I love sitting on the bleachers and watching him go.

In track, you have distance, speed, and strength events occurring throughout the meet. I find the sprinting events most interesting to watch. Every sprinter has the same routine. Prior to the event's beginning, the sprinters gather together, stretching and preparing to run the race. Some jump up and down, some sit and stretch their legs, others just stand and stare. Preparation before the race is key. Each one has a lane, and each one kneels down to set his or her feet into the starter's block, just as we've seen in the pictures from the Olympics.

Everyone is prepared, and then, all of a sudden, things get really quiet. A hush even spreads through the spectators in the stadium as the sprinters listen for the commands of the starter. They are focused, quiet, and ready to hear the gun fire, so they can run the race, and run as fast as they can.

BANG!

The gun is off, and to this day, I have never seen a runner just kneel and never get out of the blocks. They always start running, and most of the time, everyone finishes the race.

As leaders, we're a lot like those sprinters. We prepare and we're focused. Not a problem. But do we kneel down in the blocks waiting to hear the Head Starter give us the command to run the race? Do we prepare for the right race? And are we focused on the race itself, or the starter who gives the command to run the race? It's interesting to note that in high school track, it only takes one false start, jumping ahead of the command, to be disqualified.

And what about us? Do we jump ahead to run the race without hearing the gun? In life, work, and ministry, John R. Mott tells us we must put out all selfish ambition that hinders us from hearing God. And Scripture backs him up. Consider Proverbs 3:5–6: "Trust in the Lord with all your heart, and do not lean on your own understanding; in all your ways acknowledge Him, and He will make your paths straight" (NASB). In other words, we can't jump the gun. We must wait for the great Head Starter to tell us where we are to go, whom to go to, and how to get there.

Hearing God's Voice

Every day, we must ask Jesus Christ to speak to us, and we must make time to listen. Samuel understood this when he said, "Speak Lord, for your servant is listening" (1 Sam. 3:9 NASB). If we are going to unleash the power of the Almighty God and do amazing, impacting work in life and in ministry, we must tune in. We must be attentive to the Creator of the Universe. Yes, I'm saying we must listen and hear God's voice. Yes, it's hard. Yes, it's the only way to run the race. And it's the only way to accomplish God–honoring ministry.

Listening is hard! It takes time. It takes a focus that requires attention on others rather than on ourselves.

Fil Anderson says, "Listening is the greatest gift you can give someone." So are we waiting to listen to God? Ready to jump into action on His command to go wherever He says go, do what He commands us to do?

No doubt, the question that comes up is just how we're supposed to be like Samuel, and how we can say, "Speak Lord, for Your servant is listening"? Ever wonder what God's voice sounds like, looks like, tastes like, or even smells like? Chris Rice, a contemporary Christian singer, writes that hearing God is like smelling the color number nine. He sings:

> I would take "no" for an answer
> Just to know I heard You speak
> And I'm wonderin' why I've never
> Seen the signs they claim they see
> Are the special revelations
> Meant for everybody but me?
> Maybe I don't truly know you
> Or maybe I simply believe . . .
> But my heart of faith keeps poundin'
> So I know I'm doin' fine
> But sometimes finding You
> Is just like trying to
> Smell the color nine

As Mott urges, we must shun all other noises and work to be attentive to God speaking: "Listen more to God and speak less yourself," he says. "We are so noisy and busy, we don't hear God and understand His purposes."

I, like Mott, believe God speaks. Scripture testifies that He will speak into our hearts. He will give us direction, and we must not lean on our own understanding, but lean on the One who knows it all, our Lord, Jesus Christ. But yes, it is something like smelling the color nine. (As Chris Rice says, "There's no color number nine and number nine doesn't smell." His point exactly.)

If we were to lead under the direction of Christ, then, we would not be operating under our own selfish ambition. Oswald Chambers writes in his classic devotion, *My Utmost for His Highest:*

> The goal of my spiritual life is such close identification with Jesus Christ that I will always hear God and know that God always hears me (see John 11:41). If I'm united with Jesus Christ, I hear God all the time through the devotion of hearing.

Chambers continues to say that other areas of life can hinder our listening ability and divert our attention, taking our devotion away from God. I need to be devoted to the right things in life, abandoned to Christ.

In the Old Testament, 1 Samuel, chapter 3 gives us a picture of how to be attentive to God and listen to His voice. There are two areas I'd like to explore here, in hopes of helping you develop the discipline of being attentive to God. They are the preparation of the heart and the quieting of the heart. Exploring these two areas will get us on track to be leaders who tune in to God's voice. And that way, we will indeed be able to boldly and confidently say, "Speak Lord, for your servant is listening."

Preparation of the Heart

The Boy Scouts have a saying, "Be Prepared." Why? Because in life, the unexpected always happens. The Boy Scouts are focused on being outdoors and living the great adventure, which always brings the unexpected. They learn all aspects of living outdoors:

fire building, first aid, open fire cooking, orienteering, and even how to aid someone who has been bitten by a snake. They're prepared! In the same way, the first step in attention to God and hearing His voice is to be prepared. Prepare your heart. Samuel prepared his heart by ministering to the Lord. The Scriptures tell us in 1 Samuel 3:1 that Samuel did the right things and was pleasing to God. He grew in stature, following the decrees of the Lord. For us, there's only one place in which we are right with God, and that is in Jesus Christ.

> **"Come just as you are into the presence of this Christ,** be your thought of Him what it may, and resolve that you will do what He suggests that you do with reference to your character, with reference to your relation to others, no matter how difficult it is. Break out into duty, and I pledge you you will soon break out into song."[2]   **JRM**

To be prepared as a servant, then, we are to look to Him, pray to Him, and call His name in everything we think, do, and say. But we also need to think like Him. As Paul writes in Philippians 2:5–8, we must have an attitude like Christ.

> Your attitude should be the same as that of Christ Jesus:
> Who being in very nature God,
> did not consider equality with God
> something to be grasped,
> but made Himself nothing,
> taking the very nature of a servant,
> being made in human likeness.
> And being found in appearance as a man,
> He humbled himself
> and became obedient
> to death—even death on a cross (NIV).

Christ was selfless; He was a humble servant, even sacrificing His life, so we might have life and life to the fullest. Paul pushes us to have this type of attitude.

Of the Same Mind

So, are we preparing and practicing what God has called us to do? He calls us to be of the same mind as Christ, serving, loving, and giving of ourselves to others. Preparation and doing right in the sight of God, then, is to daily yield our will to Jesus Christ and adopt His attitude. Taking on the attitude of Christ is a constant battle. In work and in life, there are so many situations begging for my selfish desire to poke its ugly head out and show itself. We must practice the disciplines of prayer, then, meditating and understanding Scripture and service to others in order to become more like Christ.

Many mornings when I roll out of bed, there's a spark in my soul. But there are times when I roll over—common practice for the majority of us—and hit the snooze button, not quite ready to take on the world. To overcome this urge to snooze, I have incorporated a preparation, a practice of saying a short prayer (the first of many) to get my attitude straight with God. It goes like this:

> Lord Jesus Christ,
> Help me to yield to Your ways
> Help me to have an attitude like You.
> I need Your power to serve
> Help me to be what You would be—if You were me!

In addition, I have memorized Hebrews 12:1–2 and say it as a prayer:

> . . . Let us throw off everything that hinders and the sin that so easily entangles, and let us run with perseverance the race marked out for us. Let us fix our eyes on Jesus, the author and perfecter of our faith (NIV).

This practice is just like when I come home after every workday and give my wife a thirty-second hug. I hold on for the duration of the thirty seconds, not letting go, telling her of my love for her. This sets the whole mood between us for the evening; it sets my attitude toward her and makes her feel loved and valued. This is what I'm doing with Jesus—I wake up, giving him a thirty-second hug (just the beginning)—reminding myself who is the focus, whom I love, and who loves me.

I'm preparing for the day. I'm gearing up first thing in the morning to be attentive to God. I want to lead like Christ, love like Christ, serve like Christ. J. Oswald Sanders, in his book, *Spiritual Leadership* (one I highly recommend for everyone who wants to be a spiritual leader) tells us that God prepares leaders with a specific place and task in mind.

So we wake up every morning and prepare to do what God wants us to do, knowing He has a specific task that day for us to accomplish. Do we put on the face of Christ even after a restless night without sleep? Do we pray and ask Christ to help us, lead us, and direct us every single day? Are we aware that Christ is with us ready to point to a certain direction, person, or place? Be prepared! Before we run the race, we need to stretch, jump up and down, warm up, get our minds and our hearts ready. We never know when God will speak, and I would hate to miss the opportunity when the great Head Starter says "Go"!

So How Do We Do It?

On a practical level, here's a simple list to help us be ready to hear God and be the servants we are called to be.

- Memorize Scripture—Remember G.I.G.O. (Garbage In, Garbage Out). What are you filling your heart and soul with? Is it edifying to

Jesus? Would Jesus approve? What's in the heart comes out! Read Matthew 12:33–37.

- Set time for ten to twenty minutes of prayer every morning to prepare your soul.

- Ask for wisdom every day. I ask at least ten to twenty times throughout the day. I need it, and it keeps me focused on Him. When I go into a meeting or take a break from a stressful meeting, I ask for the Wise One to fill me up.

- Cleanse your soul by asking forgiveness. Be specific; remember Jesus gives us grace and will forgive. This act is like taking a shower and cleaning up for the party that day.

- Intentionally serve someone. Write a note of encouragement every day to someone in your organization. This forces your heart to think of someone other than yourself.

- Have someone in your office, a colleague, or friend hold you accountable to a Christlike attitude. Nurture this relationship; we need truth tellers in our lives.

- Pray for someone every day. Make a list. Put it on your computer, and change it out every month. Again, this gets the focus off of you and onto your neighbor.

- Take a walk—alone—and pray in the middle of the day. Walk around outside your office, just for a few minutes to readjust your attitude, to fix your eyes on Jesus.

- While driving, turn off the radio. Pray at every stoplight or listen to a worship CD.

When we practice simple acts like these every day, it helps prepare our hearts and sets us up to be attentive to God. But it takes practice and discipline. It's an all-encompassing feat, but we must do it if we expect to hear God speak.

Discipline in Everyday Life

Let's talk a little bit more about the discipline of it all. All leaders must have "right" disciplines in their lives.

Sanders, speaking about discipline, tells us, "Without this essential quality, all other gifts remain as dwarfs: They cannot grow. So discipline appears first on our list. Before we can conquer the world, we must first conquer the self."

In addition, Romans 12:1–2 from *The Message* says:

> So here's what I want you to do, God helping you: Take your everyday, ordinary life—your sleeping, eating, going-to-work, and walking-around life—and place it before God as an offering. Embracing what God does for you is the best thing you can do for him. Don't become so well–adjusted to your culture that you fit into it without even thinking. Instead, fix your attention on God. You'll be changed from the inside out. Readily recognize what He wants from you, and quickly respond to it. Unlike the culture around you, always dragging you down to its level of immaturity, God brings the best out of you, develops well-formed maturity in you.

In other words: Prepare! Prepare! Your everyday, ordinary life! For the race is here and we cannot hide. No, we must run. But first and foremost, we must train—train the heart, so that when God speaks, we will listen!

Quieting the Heart

We're quiet when someone is talking. It's quiet during a movie. We're quiet in church. And it finally gets quiet at my house around eleven at night, when we all sigh and sink into our beds. Quiet has some great qualities to it. But at the same time, many of us can be scared to death of the quiet, and we never make time for it.

Regardless, the quiet is where we must go. In order for us to hear God's voice, we must "Be still and know that I am God," as we're told in Psalm 46:10 (NKJV). God speaks through the gentle quietness of our hearts.

In 1 Samuel 3:3, it says: "Samuel was lying down in the temple of the Lord where the ark of God was" (NASB). Samuel was in a position to hear God's voice. He was still. He was lying down in the closest place possible to God. He was quiet. Samuel was ready to hear the call of the Lord. Maybe not expecting the voice of God to speak, but he was ready.

Do we take our position lying down patiently in the hopes that God might direct us? I don't know about you, but it seems like I'm on the treadmill of life and I can't get off, let alone be still. An essential practice for those who claim to follow Jesus, then, is to become quiet and shut everything (of this worldly life) out. And then, like the sprinter, we're to get in position, into blocks, waiting, focused and ready to hear the starter's commands to go. If we're going to do God-inspired feats, positioning ourselves near God has to be a habit in our lives.

Simply Being Silent

I meet with some men every other week, and we talk, discuss things, and pray for one another. Well, one day, one of my friends encouraged us to take a retreat in order to practice this thing called solitude: being silent, with no talking. Just listening to God. "Be silent? For how long? I can't sit still for that long! Solitude? What for?" Those were cries from my mouth. "How long? Twenty-four hours!? What will I do for twenty-four hours? No TV, no music, no remote control? You gotta be kidding!" But he wasn't.

We managed to all make it to the lake house and started this adventure of being quiet all day long and through the night. The first thirty minutes were like monkeys going from tree to tree, dancing in my head, with so much going on in my mind. But after lying down, the monkeys eventually left. And all that was before me was my heart and my God. I was exposed and my sin appeared. I asked for forgiveness, but more came to me and God's grace kept flowing over me like the waves at the ocean never stopping. They just kept coming. It was hard to face my sins, but God knew what I needed. My heart grew still. I focused on His Word, and I came into the quiet of the Lord. I just listened, and He spoke.

He spoke through my heart, through Scripture, answering my cries and my questions. I won't say I heard an audible voice; I heard God speak to me in the quietness of the heart, that place that's deep inside of the soul. My soul was nourished and renewed, and I felt revived and strengthened. It was a vacation for the soul, like I had come out of a twenty-four-hour massage, loose and relaxed, confident that I was in the midst of God's will.

Henri Nouwen says, "Solitude is the furnace that transforms the heart." And that's what it felt like! But I want my heart to be transformed every single day. I can't say that if you practice solitude every week or every month you will be transformed. But just like strength training, if you're consistent, you will see the difference. Sometimes I have great workouts; other times not so great. But I did it, and I can see the difference. The same is true with our souls: we need to exercise the soul, and we do this through lying down near God in the quiet.

You might say "I'm a doer," or "I'm a connector." Maybe it's, "I'm very social," or "I'm very busy with things to do." Maybe, "No time to waste," or "I'm just too darn busy doing great things for my community!" Fil Anderson, writer and speaker, once said, "We need to be a 'Human Being' rather than a 'Human Doer.'" Yes, we need to act and do things that make a difference, but first we need to just "be." We need to sit at the feet of Jesus, just as Mary did in Luke 10:39. She was just being. Be in the presence of the Lord.

Recognizing the Voice

Busyness, noise, and being in a hurry can stunt our spiritual growth, and we must be aware of the trap. We must make an intentional effort to *stop* and be still. Too often, when I ask friends and colleagues how they are doing, their first response is, "I'm busy, real busy," as if it's a badge of honor. But in light of Jesus, I think we have that backwards. As Mary sat at the feet of Jesus, Martha was busy doing other things and got frustrated. She was doing, and Mary was being. Jesus said Mary had chosen what was better: being at His feet.

> **"No personality becomes real unless one has knowledge** of that personality. My friend is real to me. . . . If Christ is to be real to us we must have confidence in His character, life, and power."[3]   **JRM**

Servant leaders understand this, and they take time to do nothing but be quiet. They have to nourish the soul, to serve like Jesus would serve. If we are going to hear God speak, we have to get accustomed to the practice of quiet and solitude, of being still.

When my wife—or even a longtime friend—calls me on the phone, I recognize the voice immediately because I have nurtured that relationship. I've logged many hours of listening to their voices. I've spent time with them, and I know them. Do you know God's voice? Could you recognize it? It begins with quiet—sitting at the feet of Jesus.

We hear God's voice through many avenues. We hear His voice through other people of faith who speak truth. We hear God's voice through Scripture. Scripture is God's Word, and He communicated His commands and direction through the Holy Word. Jesus also promised the Holy Spirit to help us discern what is true and what is not. In the quiet and stillness of the Lord, He leads us to people, He leads us to His Word, and He leads by the Holy Spirit. He leads us to act but only in the quiet of our hearts.

According to John 10:3–4, Jesus said, "He calls His own sheep by name and leads them out . . . the sheep [us]

follow Him because they know His voice" (NASB). And John the Baptist, according to John 3:29, said, "The friend who attends the bridegroom waits and listens for him and is full of joy when he hears the bridegroom's voice" (NIV).

Hearing at the Holy Land

Mott himself knew the joy of waiting and listening. He would routinely retreat with other men, as well as go to the Holy Land. He writes:

> On my last visit to the Holy Land I went out alone to revisit the Mount of Olives. I was prompted to make a pilgrimage as in my morning meditation there broke upon me more powerfully than ever these words "He went, as His custom was to the Mount of Olives." Take note—out of the busy city, out of the noisy city, out of the crowded city, out of the sin-bound city, out to the zone of silence under the peaceful olive tree—there to meditate, to be attentive unto God, to hold unhurried communion with His Heavenly Father.

He goes on to say:

> . . . if our blessed Lord Who is our perfect example in everything else found it necessary, or desirable, thus to hold unhurried and responsive fellowship with the Heavenly Father, what presumptuous and alarming folly for us to assume that in these busy, noisy lives of ours [nothing has changed!] and in the midst of the dangerous cross-currents of this modern world, we can do without.

It's folly if we, as leaders, ignore the practice of quiet and communion with the Heavenly Father. If we're going to direct, then we need to allow our souls to be directed.

Rob Bell, on his DVD, *NOOMA Noise*, asks these penetrating questions that we must ask ourselves:

- Why is silence so hard to deal with?
- When was the last time you were in a solitary place?
- Does my schedule, my time, my life look like that of a person who wants to hear God's voice?
- Do you believe God's voice is more interesting than voices around you?
- Is there a connection between the amount of noise in our lives and our inability to hear God?
- Have you spent the same amount of time worrying and talking about your difficult, confusing situations as you have spent in silence listening to what God might have to say?

In pondering these things, we must keep in mind the importance of quieting the heart. And here are a few suggestions for doing just that:

- Take thirty minutes each day to be still, wait, and listen for God's voice.
- Find a place where you can quiet your heart. Go often to this place.
- Take a half-day of solitude, just being quiet and reading God's Word. Do this once or twice a year. Schedule the time in your planner.
- Develop "truth–tellers" in your life, people who will speak honestly. When you feel God speaking, test it with the "truth-tellers." Eli did this for Samuel in 1 Samuel 3:5–9.

Finally, in closing, I'd like to share a few comments from Salvation Army evangelist Commissioner Samuel Logan Brengle, speaking on his spiritual disciplines:

> I do a lot of listening. Prayer, you know, is not meant to be a monologue, but a dialogue. It is a communion, a friendly talk. While the Lord communicates with me mainly through His Word, He gives me a great deal of comfort in a direct manner. By "comfort" I

do not mean cuddling or coddling, but assurance—assurance of His presence with me and His pleasure in my service. It's like the comfort given by a military commander to his soldier or envoy whom he sends on a difficult mission: "You go, put on your armor, I'm watching you, and I'll send you all the reinforcements you need as they are needed." I have to be comforted that way a great deal. I don't assume that God is near me and pleased with me; I must have a fresh witness daily.

I believe that if we prepare our hearts and seek quiet, we'll find direction, peace, joy, and courage to lead an organization to the place in which we can please the Father. Don't we all want the Creator of the universe to say, "Well done, good and faithful servant"? I'm convinced these are the exact words Mott heard from his Heavenly Father, since he was attentive to God and boldly said daily: "Speak, Lord, for your servant is listening." The results speak for themselves.

"Be still before the Lord, and wait patiently for him" (Ps. 37:7 NRSV).

LESSON 15
IN REFLECTION

For Yourself

1. How does listening to God impact you at your workplace?
2. Do you run to God's quieting power only in times of crisis or conflict?
3. What tangible benefits could come out of these disciplines that strengthen your leadership capabilities?
4. What selfish ambitions do you need to give up in order to hear God's voice?
5. Listening is the greatest gift you can give someone. When did you last give this gift to God?

For Group Discussion and Leadership

1. What activities in your organization take your focus away from God?
2. How do busyness, noise, and hurry stunt the growth of your organization?
3. How does an organization prepare its heart to be attentive to God?
4. List practical steps your organization can take to develop discipline in being attentive to God.

CONTRIBUTORS

Sean Allison serves as president and CEO of the Manatee County YMCA. He began his YMCA career in his hometown of Springfield, Missouri, and has served YMCA associations in Owensboro and Glasgow, Kentucky; Charlotte, North Carolina; and St. Louis, Missouri. After years in coaching, Sean answered God's call to serve Jesus Christ through the YMCA. He is a cofounder of the Dunamis Newsletter and the YMCA John 17:21 Conference. A graduate of Drury University, he, his wife Colleen, and their children: Meghan, Sam, Hank, Jack, Ocean, and Nate, live in Bradenton, Florida.

Jack Bender is a management consultant with the YMCA of the USA and serves twenty-eight corporate YMCAs in North Carolina. Jack has thirty-six years of YMCA experience ranging from working in programs for youth to being the CEO of a midsize YMCA in Knoxville, Tennessee. Jack has a B.S. from Abilene Christian University and an M.H.R.D. from University Associates, San Diego, California.

Wesley Bender serves as director at the Jay Levergood Teen Center in Alpharetta, Georgia. This state-of-the-art teen center works hand in hand with the Ed Isakson/Alpharetta Family YMCA just outside of Atlanta. Wes has a deep love for today's young people and loves to program activities that allow a diversity of youth to get out of their comfort zones, learn more about their God-given talents, and give those gifts back to the community. Wesley has a B.A. from Lipscomb University.

161

David Byrd is the chief operating officer for the YMCA of Middle Tennessee. Prior to his work in Nashville, David served as CEO of the Durham YMCA, North Carolina, and held positions in Orlando and Jacksonville, Florida, and Charlotte, North Carolina. David holds an M.S. degree from the University of North Carolina and earned his B.S. at High Point University. He and his wife, Jan, have two daughters, Kasie and Sara, and four grandchildren, Dylan, Kaylee, Baxter Elizabeth, and Averie.

Eric Ellsworth is chief operating officer/executive vice president of the YMCA of Greater Charlotte in Charlotte, North Carolina, the eighth largest YMCA in the United States. Prior to working in Charlotte, Eric was the CEO of the YMCA of Southwestern Indiana, serving a five county area in Southern Indiana. Eric began his YMCA career in Madisonville, Kentucky, and he has served the YMCA mission since 1976. A native of Indiana, he completed his undergraduate degree at Western Kentucky University and his master's degree at Springfield College. He and his wife, Karen, have two children: Whitney, twenty-four, and Leif, twenty-two.

W. Tracy Howe is a senior vice president of operations for the YMCA of the Triangle. He has worked in various roles in the YMCA for the past twenty-three years. For the past eight years, Tracy has chaired the John 17:21 Conference, a spiritual renewal conference for YMCA directors. A graduate of Purdue University, Tracy lives in Cary, North Carolina, with his wife, Pamela, and three children: Ryan, Austin, and Kylie.

Tim Joyce is senior vice president of operations at the YMCA of the Triangle. He has held various leadership positions with the YMCA over the course of his nineteen-year career. Tim's background includes camp work with youth. He has a B.S. in business administration from the University of North Carolina at Chapel Hill.

Doug Kohl is President and CEO of the Akron Area YMCA in Ohio. A career YMCA professional, he has been involved with the YMCA since he was eight years old. Doug's YMCA program background includes youth work, physical education, and camping. He earned a bachelor's degree in physical education from George Williams College and his master's degree in business management from Aurora University. He and his wife, Kathy, have three children, Stephanie, Zachary, and Kaitlyn.

Jay W. Lippy serves as chaplain for the Tampa Metro YMCA. Jay volunteered in the association for several years before accepting the position of executive director for YMCA Camp Cristina in 1995 while completing his senior program director certification. He is a veteran of the U.S. Navy, member of the Downtown Tampa Rotary Club, and a founding member of the John 17:21 Conference. Jay is also a regular speaker at national and international YMCA conferences and serves as pastor for a congregation in Tampa. Jay has an A.A. in music and a B.A. in theology. Jay and his wife of twenty-seven years, Phyl, have three children and two grandsons.

Dick Marks retired from the YMCA after thirty-five years, thirty of which were serving as an executive director. He has held top leadership positions in church and community organizations and is the father of five children. Dick is a regular contributor to the Association of YMCA Professionals' (AYP) journal, *Perspective*. He earned his B.A. from Northeastern University and an M.B.A. from Frostburg University.

Tom Massey is the CEO of Triangle2 Partners, a professional service firm serving nonprofit organizations. Tom spent twenty years as a YMCA professional, both in Arkansas and Florida, and for the YMCA of the USA. He has B.S. and M.S. degrees and has completed course work on a Ph.D. in health and human services. Tom is a member of the *USA Today* Baby Boomer Panel and responds to contemporary societal issues for the international newspaper.

Paul McEntire is the president and COO of the YMCA of Florida's First Coast in Jacksonville, Florida. Paul has worked for the YMCA for nine years. Paul was previously a pastor for twelve years in the suburbs of Chicago. He has a bachelor's degree in business administration from the University of Illinois and a master of divinity degree from the Southern Baptist Theological Seminary.

Nancy Reece is senior vice president of leadership development at the YMCA of Middle Tennessee and has held various leadership positions over her twenty-plus-year career with the YMCA. She has a B.A. from the University of Evansville and an M.S. from Indiana University. She writes a column for the Association of YMCA Professionals' journal, *Perspective*.

Craig Seibert lives in Charlotte, North Carolina, and works full time with Priority Associates, the marketplace ministry of Campus Crusade for Christ. He also serves as the Christian Focus Coordinator for the YMCA of Greater Charlotte and the project leader on the YMCA Mission Web site. Craig received B.S. and M.S. degrees from Purdue University and was ordained through the International Ministerial Fellowship.

Lori Swann is currently a partner with Triangle2 Partners, offering leadership in marketing, communications, research, and business planning to the firm's portfolio. She worked for fifteen years with the YMCA of Middle Tennessee in a variety of roles including branch executive, vice president of marketing, and senior vice president of operations. A graduate of Middle Tennessee State University with a degree in mass communications and public relations, Lori also has an M.B.A. from Vanderbilt University.

Burnie Whitson serves on the staff of the YMCA of the USA as a management consultant to twenty-seven YMCAs in South Carolina and Georgia. His twenty-five-year tenure in the YMCA includes nineteen years as the CEO of the Pickens County YMCA. He received his B.S. degree from Winthrop University, where he met his wife, Jan. He and Jan live in Easley, South Carolina, with their four children, Megan, Briley, Kelsey, and Tanner.

NOTES
For Highlighted Quotes by John R. Mott

Chapter 1

1. "The Leadership for the Coming Day," in *Five Decades and a Forward View* (New York and London: Harper & Brothers, 1939), 132.
2. Ibid., 133.
3. "Bible Study for Spiritual Growth," address to students at Lahore, India, January 1896. From *Addresses and Papers of John R. Mott, Volume VI: Selected Papers and Addresses on Evangelistic, Spiritual, and Ecumenical Subjects and the Outreach of Life and Influence* (New York: Association Press, 1947), 104.

Chapter 2

1. "The Christian Message," in the appendix of *The Present-Day Summons to the World Mission of Christianity* (Nashville, Tenn.: Cokesbury Press, 1931), 239.
2. "The Secret of Liberating a Greater Christina Force," in *Liberating the Lay Forces of Christianity: The Ayer Lectures for 1931* (New York, N.Y.: The Macmilllan Company, 1932), 119.

Chapter 3

1. "Lessons I Have Learned Over Fifty Years of Helping to Establish National and World-wide Christian Movements," given at Rochester, New York, 1943, and at Lake Geneva, Wisconsin and Silver Bay, New York, 1944, to groups of association secretaries. In *Addresses and Papers of John R. Mott, Volume VI: Selected Papers and Addresses on Evangelistic, Spiritual, and Ecumenical Subjects and the Outreach of Life and Influence* (New York, N.Y.: Association Press, 1947), 526.

Chapter 5

1. "Bible Study for Spiritual Growth," 103.
2. Ibid., 104.
3. Ibid., 103.
4. Ibid., 102.

Chapter 6

1. "Outlines Employed in the Coaching of Workers." From *Addresses and Papers of John R. Mott, Volume VI: Selected Papers and*

Addresses on Evangelistic, Spiritual, and Ecumenical Subjects and the Outreach of Life and Influence (New York: Association Press, 1947), 503.

2. "The Secret Prayer-Life," address to students at Calcutta, India, 1896. From *Addresses and Papers of John R. Mott, Volume VI: Selected Papers and Addresses on Evangelistic, Spiritual, and Ecumenical Subjects and the Outreach of Life and Influence* (New York: Association Press, 1947), 111.

3. Ibid.

Chapter 7

1. "Lessons I Have Learned Over Fifty Years of Helping to Establish National and World-wide Christian Movements," given at Rochester, New York, 1943, and at Lake Geneva, Wisconsin and Silver Bay, New York, 1944 to groups of association secretaries. From *Addresses and Papers of John R. Mott, Volume VI: Selected Papers and Addresses on Evangelistic, Spiritual, and Ecumenical Subjects and the Outreach of Life and Influence* (New York: Association Press, 1947), 525.

Chapter 8

1. "Co-operation and the World Mission," 1945. From *Addresses and Papers of John R. Mott, Volume VI: Selected Papers and Addresses on Evangelistic, Spiritual, and Ecumenical Subjects and the Outreach of Life and Influence* (New York: Association Press, 1947), 485.

2. "Lessons I Have Learned," 525.

3. "The Secret of Liberating a Greater Christian Force," in *Liberating the Lay Forces of Christianity: The Ayer Lectures for 1931* (New York: The Macmillan Company, 1932), 116.

Chapter 9

1. "The Present World Situation," address at the meeting of the General Assembly of the Church of Scotland, Edinburgh, 1930. From *Addresses and Papers of John R. Mott, Volume VI: Selected Papers and Addresses on Evangelistic, Spiritual, and Ecumenical Subjects and the Outreach of Life and Influence* (New York: Association Press, 1947), 243.

2. *The Present-Day Summons to the World Mission of Christianity* (Nashville, Tenn.: Cokesbury Press, 1931), 239.

3. "Co-operation and the World Mission," 463.

Chapter 10

1. "Outlines Employed in the Coaching of Workers," 504.
2. "The Leadership for the Coming Day," 128–29.

Chapter 4

1. "The Secret of Liberating a Greater Christian Force," 115.
2. Ibid., 114–15.

Chapter 2

1. "The Christian Message," from the appendix of *The Present-Day Summons to the World Mission of Christianity* (Nashville, Tenn.: Cokesbury Press, 1931), 239.
2. "The Secret of Liberating a Greater Christian Force," 119.

Chapter 3

1. "Lessons I Have Learned," 525.
2. Ibid.

Chapter 11

1. "Individual Work for Individuals," taken from the volume *The Larger Evangelism* (Nashville, Tenn.: Abingdon-Cokesbury Press, 1944) from *Addresses and Papers of John R. Mott, Volume VI: Selected Papers and Addresses on Evangelistic, Spiritual, and Ecumenical Subjects and the Outreach of Life and Influence* (New York: Association Press, 1947), 82.
2. "The Secret of Liberating a Greater Christian Force," 127.
3. "Suggestions for Character Building," address given at a student mass meeting, Shanghai, China, 1913. From *Addresses and Papers of John R. Mott, Volume VI: Selected Papers and Addresses on Evangelistic, Spiritual, and Ecumenical Subjects and the Outreach of Life and Influence* (New York: Association Press, 1947), 150.

Chapter 12

1. "The Secret of Liberating a Greater Christian Force," 107.
2. *The Present-Day Summons to the World Mission of Christianity* (Nashville, Tenn.: Cokesbury Press, 1931), 241.
3. "The Secret of Liberating a Greater Christian Force," 131–32.

Chapter 13

1. "The Use of Time," address at Stellenbosch University, South Africa, 1934. From *Addresses and Papers of John R. Mott, Volume VI:*

Notes

169

Selected Papers and Addresses on Evangelistic, Spiritual, and Ecumenical Subjects and the Outreach of Life and Influence (New York: Association Press, 1947), 215.

Chapter 14

1. "The Use of Time," 217.
2. Ibid., 215.
3. Ibid.

Chapter 15

1. "How May Jesus Christ Become a Reality to Me?" address at Oxford University, Oxford, England, February 1905. From *Addresses and Papers of John R. Mott, Volume VI: Selected Papers and Addresses on Evangelistic, Spiritual, and Ecumenical Subjects and the Outreach of Life and Influence* (New York: Association Press, 1947), 100–101.

2. "Religion Primarily a Matter of the Will," address given at the University of Halle, Germany, April 1899. From *Addresses and Papers of John R. Mott, Volume VI: Selected Papers and Addresses on Evangelistic, Spiritual, and Ecumenical Subjects and the Outreach of Life and Influence* (New York: Association Press, 1947), 58.

3. "How May Jesus Christ Become a Reality to Me?" address at Oxford University, Oxford, England, February 1905. From *Addresses and Papers of John R. Mott, Volume VI: Selected Papers and Addresses on Evangelistic, Spiritual, and Ecumenical Subjects and the Outreach of Life and Influence* (New York: Association Press, 1947), 94.

SELECTED BIBLIOGRAPHY

Anderson, Fil. *Running on Empty: Contemplative Spirituality for Overachievers.* Colorado Springs, Colo.: WaterBrook Press, 2004.

Bell, Rob. *NOOMA Noise.* DVD. Grand Rapids, Mich.: Zondervan, 2005.

Buechner, Frederick. *The Sacred Journey.* San Francisco, Calif.: Harper & Row Publishers, 1982.

Chambers, Oswald. *My Utmost for His Highest.* Grand Rapids, Mich.: Oswald Chambers Publications, 1992.

Hopkins, C. Howard. *John R. Mott: 1865–1955.* Grand Rapids, Mich.: William B. Eerdmans Publishing Company, 1979.

Hybels, Bill. *The Volunteer Revolution: Unleashing the Power of Everybody.* Grand Rapids, Mich.: Zondervan, 2004.

Kilgore, Randall. *Calm My Storm, Lord: Real World Studies for Finding Wholeness in Your Workplace.* Boston, Mass.: Marketplace Network, 1999.

McMenamin, Cindi. *When Women Long for Rest: God's Peace for Your Overwhelmed Life.* Eugene, Ore.: Harvest House Publishers, 2004.

Nouwen, Henri. *The Only Necessary Thing.* New York, N.Y.: Crossroad Publishing, 1999.

———. *The Way of the Heart.* New York, N.Y.: Ballantine Books, 1981.

Oswalt, John. *The Leisure Crisis.* Wheaton, Ill.: Victor Books, 1987.

Perkins, Spencer and Chris Rice. *More than Equals: Racial Healing for the Sake of the Gospel.* Downers Grove, Ill.: InterVarsity Press, 2000.

Rice, Chris. *Smell the Color 9.* Rocketown Records LLC. 2000. CD.

Sanders, J. Oswald. *Spiritual Leadership.* Chicago, Ill.: Moody Press, 1994.

Warren, Rick. The Purpose-Driven Life. Grand Rapids, Mich.: Zondervan, 2002.

SELECTED WORKS OF JOHN R. MOTT

John R. Mott was a prolific writer and speaker. A full bibliography of all his books, speeches, articles, and personal correspondence would be difficult to compile. The following titles are those we found most helpful in developing *Strengthening the Organizational Heart.*

1897

Strategic Points in the World's Conquest: The Universities and Colleges as Related to the Progress of Christianity. New York, Chicago: F. H. Revell Company.

1900

The Evangelization of the World in This Generation. New York, N. Y.: Student Volunteer Movement for Foreign Missions.

1904

The Pastor and Modern Missions: A Plea for Leadership in World Evangelization. New York. N. Y.: Student Volunteer Movement for Foreign Missions.

1908

The Future Leadership of the Church. New York, N. Y.: Young Men's Christian Association.

1910

The Decisive Hour of Christian Missions. New York, N. Y.: Student Volunteer Movement for Foreign Missions.

1911

The Claims and Opportunities of the Christian Ministry. New York, N. Y.: Young Men's Christian Association Press.

1920

The World's Student Christian Federation: Origin, Achievements, Forecast; Achievements of the First Quarter-Century of the World's Student Christian Federation and Forecast of Unfinished Tasks. London: World's Student Christian Federation.

1923

Confronting Young Men with the Living Christ. New York, N. Y.: Association Press.

1925

The Moslem World of To-Day. New York, N. Y.: George H. Doran Company.

1931

The Present-Day Summons to the World Mission of Christianity. Nashville, Tenn.: Cokesbury Press.

1932

Liberating the Lay Forces of Christianity: The Ayer Lectures for 1931. New York, N. Y.: The Macmillan Company.

1935

Cooperation and the World Mission. New York, N. Y.: International Missionary Council.

1938

Evangelism for the World Today, As Interpreted By Christian Leaders Throughout the World. New York and London: Published for The International Missionary Council by Harper & Brothers.

1939

Five Decades and A Forward View. New York and London, Harper & Brothers.

1939

Methodists United For Action. Nashville, Tenn.: Dept. of Education and Promotion, Board of Missions, Methodist Church.

1944

The Larger Evangelism. New York, N. Y.: Abingdon-Cokesbury Press.

1946–47

Addresses and Papers of John R. Mott: Selected Papers and Addresses on Evangelistic, Spiritual, and Ecumenical Subjects and the Outreach of Life and Influence. 6 vols. New York, N. Y.: Association Press.